TESTIMONIALS

Barbara Greenspan Shaiman has a passion for young people and for creating meaningful connections between generations. She has a wonderful story to tell about how people can become involved in their communities and help others, while becoming better people themselves. I can think of no better way, especially at this time in America's history, to reach out to the next generation. Through networking and encouraging others to volunteer, she has created a model for anyone looking for a way to give something back to society.

Andrea Mitchell,
Journalist, NBC News

Barbara Greenspan Shaiman is quite simply a pioneer and a social inventor for our times.

Harris Wofford,
former U.S. Senator, Pennsylvania

Barbara Greenspan Shaiman is a dynamo whose energy, drive, and intelligence have made a real difference here in Philadelphia. She has taught young people the value of caring and of giving back.

Edward G. Rendell,
Governor of Pennsylvania

Barbara is a remarkable individual, full of energy, with an unquenchable passion for serving others. Through her leadership, Champions of Caring has become an extraordinary force for positive change in the world.

Suzanne and Bob Wright,
Founders, Autism Speaks

Live Your Legacy Now!

Ten Simple Steps to Find
Your Passion and Change the World

Barbara Greenspan Shaiman

iUniverse, Inc.
New York   Bloomington

Live Your Legacy Now!
Ten Simple Steps to Find Your Passion and Change the World

iUniverse books may be ordered through booksellers or by contacting:

iUniverse
1663 Liberty Drive
Bloomington, IN 47403
www.iuniverse.com
1-800-Authors (1-800-288-4677)

Because of the dynamic nature of the Internet, any Web addresses or links contained in this book may have changed since publication and may no longer be valid. The views expressed in this work are solely those of the author and do not necessarily reflect the views of the publisher, and the publisher hereby disclaims any responsibility for them.

ISBN: 978-1-4401-6672-3 (pbk)
ISBN: 978-1-4401-6673-0 (cloth)
ISBN: 978-1-4401-6674-7 (ebook)

Printed in the United States of America

iUniverse rev. date: 11/2/09

DEDICATION

This book is written, with much love and gratitude:

In memory of my grandmother, Golda Greenspan; my father, Henry Greenspan; and my husband, Larry Shaiman.

In honor of my mother, Carola Greenspan, who taught me to live my life fully and with purpose.

In tribute to my brother, Joshua Greenspan; my children, Deborah and Jeremy Ryan and Daniel Eisenbud; my grandchildren, Jacob and Rebecca Ryan; and the thousands of Champions of Caring whose lives have profoundly touched my own.

ACKNOWLEDGMENTS

Live Your Legacy Now! was inspired by the lessons taught to me by my parents, Henry and Carola Greenspan, and my grandmother Golda Greenspan, who were survivors of the Holocaust. They taught me about living a life of purpose and meaning, and the importance of being a *mensch*.

My husband, Larry Shaiman, energized me to keep writing this book, even while he was fighting his battle against cancer, which he lost in January of 2009. He believed in me and supported me in all of my efforts.

Jacqueline Fearer is owed a great deal of credit for encouraging me to write this book. She was invaluable in getting me to start to record my thoughts and those of my parents, which are the soul of this book. She helped me put these words to paper.

I am indebted to Brianne Tangney, who provided me with guidance and constant support throughout the writing and editing process. Her research and assistance with this book were invaluable. She kept me organized and sane, and shares my passion for changing the world.

My son, Daniel Eisenbud, lovingly edited this manuscript, giving numerous helpful suggestions and ideas. He helped me to stay focused and present my thoughts clearly and succinctly. He is an outstanding writer and editor.

My gratitude to Margaret Moran for her encouragement and for being level-headed, supportive and always keeping me on track.

I am thankful to David and Margie Rosenberg, whose friendship and support have made my dreams a reality.

I am grateful to my daughter Deborah Ryan, for her love and support. I am proud that she and her husband Jeremy are teaching their children to become champions of caring.

Thank you to my brother, Joshua Greenspan, who helped me to reflect on the lessons learned from our family history, and who shares my passion for keeping these lessons alive.

A special thanks to my stepdaughters, Cindy Bamforth, Pamela Dumont, Shira Shaiman and their families for being a source of strength and love.

I am very grateful to the people who have touched my life and taught me so much. This list includes mentors, friends, colleagues, and the many people who helped me to create Champions of Caring, as well as the thousands of students, teachers, and administrators whom I have worked with in the greater Philadelphia region.

Contents

PART I

PART II

PREFACE

Today, the world is a profoundly troubled place. Racism, violence, and other forms of bigotry and discrimination continue to poison our relationships with one another, and among entire countries. Our communities are faced with poverty, hunger, illiteracy, teen pregnancy, and drug and alcohol abuse. Our very planet is in trouble. In the face of such abject despair, people of all ages feel helpless, isolated, and uncertain about their future. Because the challenges we face seem overwhelming, we often close our eyes—and our hearts—to the suffering around us. We don't think that we have the power to change things. *This is simply not so.*

Indeed, I am propelled by the heartfelt belief that if people realized they actually could use their passion, skills, and life lessons to make the world a better place, they would. I feel strongly that you do not have to be a celebrity, politician, powerful executive, or multi-millionaire to live and leave a meaningful legacy. It is my hope that this book will help readers of all backgrounds, ages, and life stages begin their personal journey of living their legacies—of finding the core of who they are and creating meaning in their lives by giving back.

As the daughter of Holocaust survivors, it has been my life's mission to share the universal lessons of the dangers of silence and indifference, and the importance of speaking out against injustices. What I learned from my parents' experiences is that the best response to violence and hatred is educating others about love, caring, and making a difference. My mother is the sole survivor of a family of sixty-five people, and was incarcerated in Auschwitz. My father worked for Oskar Schindler, on whose story Steven Spielberg's film "Schindler's List" was based. In 1995, after meeting Spielberg, I was inspired to create Champions of Caring (championsofcaring.org), a not-for-profit organization that has since educated and empowered over 10,000 youth in Philadelphia and South Africa to become social activists and create service projects that address societal needs.

I wrote *Live Your Legacy Now!* because I want to share how my family's history inspired me to become a social entrepreneur and use my energy and experience to create a not-for-profit organization designed to improve society. As we face these extraordinarily difficult and uncertain economic and political times, President Obama's inspirational and newly-urgent call to public service is resonating more than ever. I believe that we must all heed this call. I hope that this book will motivate readers to reflect on their own personal stories and use their skills to create meaningful change in their own lives, communities, and the world.

Barbara Greenspan Shaiman
Bala Cynwyd, Pennsylvania, 2009

Introduction

All of us have some person, event, or circumstance in our lives that shapes who we are. Like royalty, I was born with a title: Daughter of Holocaust Survivors. This was a burden that was sometimes too heavy to carry, but impossible to ignore.

My family history has shaped and influenced my life, and taught me a great deal about tragedy, humanity, and responsibility. Every day of my life, I have tried to live the legacy that my family passed onto me, and to share it with others.

But this is not a book about the Holocaust, nor is it simply my personal memoir. While a significant portion of this book details my family history, my life experiences, and the creation of Champions of Caring (the not-for-profit organization I founded in 1995), I really wrote these words to help others begin to explore their own legacies and to find what inspires them to make a difference in the world. This book is about *living your legacy*; not leaving it behind you.

It is a book for those who believe, or have a nagging suspicion, that there is something more than the lives they are currently living. It asks personal questions, such as:

- *Who are you?*
- *What is your family history?*
- *What are your core values?*
- *What are your skills and interests?*
- *What are you passionate about?*
- *What is your vision for a better world?*
- *What problem or social issue motivates you to take action?*

Through anecdotes, humor, reflection, suggestions (and maybe a little nudging), I hope to give you some answers and to motivate you to assess your core values, reflect on your life choices, and use your passion and skills to help others in order to live your legacy. This book is a primer for people who want to achieve their potential to live a richer and more meaningful life *now* and make the world a better place.

Winston Churchill once said, "We shall draw from the heart of suffering itself the means of inspiration and survival." That my parents are both Holocaust survivors instilled in me the drive to tell their stories and make a difference. But I don't expect others to tap into my same source of inspiration, or share my particular passion for working with youth. Different seeds of inspiration are all around us; we have only to look. No matter what stage of life you are in, or how much, or how little, money or time you have, this book can help you begin to *live your legacy* now.

What Do You Mean by a Legacy?

Most often, a legacy is described as something we leave behind. It is usually used in terms of money to build or fund something, such as a building at a university, a hospital wing or a library in a person's memory. But the meaning of living your legacy—your *humanity*—is much broader. I believe that a legacy is a gift to the future *and* a gift to the present. It is the core of who you are—what you stand for, how you treat others, and what you contribute to improve the world around you. You can live a legacy by the type of person you are and the way you lead your life.

Looking in the mirror is one way to see who you are, but another is to examine how you are living your life and how you are contributing to the greater good. Finding your humanity—what makes you, you— and using it to lead a meaningful life of quiet influence or passionate purpose, this is what living your legacy is about.

The process of creating a legacy is both *selfish* and *selfless*. In doing for others, we gain much more for ourselves. When we give serious thought to how we want people to view us and remember us, we can put our own stamp on our legacies. Think of it as composing your life backwards. What a great opportunity to ensure that your legacy represents your particular interests and resonates with your own style. Is that selfish? Maybe, but it's okay when you are investing so much of yourself in something so valuable. I feel that it is important to find and, yes, *flaunt* your humanity.

Who, *Me* Create a Legacy?

Celebrities, politicians, heads of state, and wealthy individuals talk about their legacies and use their influence and resources to address local and global issues. I feel strongly that every one of us can live a legacy and make a contribution. I know that this is true both because of my own experience, and because I have witnessed what people of all ages can accomplish when they are given the tools to make positive changes in their schools, communities, and the larger world. We each can use our specific talents and skills to address the issues that are most important to us. You need passion, commitment, tenacity, and a *plan*.

I know that we all face unique daily personal challenges and problems that make the prospect of changing the world even in small ways seem daunting. But what better way to get outside of our own difficult circumstances than to engage in purposeful, meaningful pursuits? In my own life, I have faced a great deal of loss, including the recent deaths of both my father and my husband while writing this book. I have found that through my work with Champions of Caring and focusing on giving back to others, I am able to get through my own pain.

About *Live Your Legacy Now!*

While this book starts with my story, and the stories of people of various ages whom I have worked with over the years, it is really about creating your own story. It is about how you can take your passion and live your legacy now. This book demonstrates how you can embrace, enjoy, and live your own legacy and fill your days with challenge and purpose.

The book is divided into two parts. The first section is about my family history; the lessons I learned as the daughter of Holocaust survivors; and how and why I started Champions of Caring. In each chapter, there are "guiding questions" that I hope will help you to reflect on your own story and life experiences and find your inspiration. I suggest that you have a notebook or journal available to respond to these important questions.

The second part of the book focuses on *you*. It provides the guidelines and the tools to help you create your own legacy through self-reflection—to take action to improve your community, and to share this experience with others. Part II begins with examples of how others are living their legacies, and then offers strategies and suggestions for living your legacy at any age or life stage—whether you are a teen, young professional, baby boomer, or retiree. Effectively utilizing your own time and resources, no matter how much of either you possess, is also discussed.

I will guide you through creating a Legacy Profile: a self-assessment tool to help you understand where you are on the path to creating your legacy. The profile asks you to reflect on your values, passions, and skills, and to determine how much time you can commit to this endeavor. Are you at the beginner level and ready to take the first steps to get involved in your community? Are you at an intermediate level, ready to create a project on your own? Or are you advanced, and eager to take on the challenge of establishing your own not-for-profit organization?

I know that getting started is the hardest part. So often we want to *do something*, but we don't know what, or how to begin. My Ten Steps will guide you through the process of either getting involved in existing projects in your community, or creating your own project. The steps will help you stay organized and gain the support of family, friends, and community members. For those of you who are ready to take on the challenge of creating your own not-for-profit organization, there is a section for you as well.

One of the most important parts of living your legacy is sharing it with others. There is a chapter that pays special attention to working with youth and engaging them in projects. I share some of the best practices that I have learned through my experiences with Champions of Caring. Following the tips in this chapter will help you to create intergenerational projects and teach young people the skills to help ensure that service becomes a way of life for them.

I also guide you through the process of writing Legacy Letters to loved ones—family, friends, colleagues—to acknowledge the important roles that these people play in your life, to reflect upon experiences that you have shared, and to motivate them to live their legacies as well.

Finally, I present the idea of creating Legacy Clubs, where you can share your legacy with others, both within your community and through social networking and online communities. This will help create a network of legacy-builders who can support one another.

So what are you waiting for?

- Dream big and start small.
- Be creative.
- Be determined.
- Be deliberate.
- Be relentless!

Now is the time to create a vision of what you want your life and your world to be. *Now* is the time to become inspired by your personal history and life experiences—to find your passion, and to use your skills to help change the world. *Now* is the time to *Live Your Legacy*.

PART I

Chapter 1. MY LEGACY

My Name Is Bella

My name is Bella, and this name means everything to me. I was named after my maternal grandmother who perished during the Holocaust. I was born on January 22, 1948 in Regensburg, Germany. When my family moved to the United States in 1951, friends told them that Bella was an immigrant name, and that I needed a strong American name. My mother, afraid that I would be stigmatized and unable to fit in with my peers, legally changed my name to Barbara. However, to this day she still calls me Bella. With this name as a daily reminder of my family legacy, I have tried to live not only my own life, but the life that was taken away from my grandmother.

When I was three-years-old, I remember seeing the numbers tattooed on the arm of my paternal grandmother Golda. "Bella," she told me, "a bad man named Hitler did this to me and you should never forget. One day, *you must do something about it.*" Obviously, as a young child, I had no idea what that something would be. It wasn't until more than forty years later that I figured it out.

My name and family history have shaped my life and driven my need to do something to teach the universal lessons of the Holocaust: to teach people that silence and indifference in the face of violence and hatred are unacceptable; that we must speak up for what we believe in;

3

and that we must make socially responsible decisions for the greater good. In order to understand the path that ultimately led me to create my own not-for-profit organization and live my legacy, you must understand where it all began. And so, this book really begins with my mother.

Carola Iserowski

My mother, Carola Iserowski, was born in Lodz, Poland, on November 11, 1921. She was the youngest of four children by nearly fifteen years. She had two brothers, Herman and Adek, and a sister, Stephanie. My mother remembers her own mother, Bella, as warm and loving. Her father Joshua was an importer of food and clothing. As a young woman, my mother became an ardent Zionist. She and her friends belonged to Bnai Akiba, a group whose goal was to foster love of Judaism and the Jewish homeland. When the war broke out, she was twenty-years-old.

My mother describes her early years in Lodz, Poland in the happiest of terms: "We had a rich cultural background and a wonderful family life." But those family ties, so strongly wound, would begin to unravel in 1939 with the German invasion of Poland. First came the ghettoization, where an entire community of Jews was walled-in and cut off from Polish society. This was Hitler's first step in a plan to dehumanize and then exterminate all Jews. My mother's stories of ghetto life are just the beginning of the nightmare that unfolded. In her words:

> *Four years in that Lodz ghetto, I lost everybody. People were dying left and right of hunger and disease because no one outside the walls cared. No one cared… There were so many orphans because the parents were deported or they died. And the little children that were left were put up in one part of the ghetto, and we youngsters were taking care of them in groups. We played with them and sang songs to recreate a little normalcy in their lives.*
>
> *I remember that black Wednesday in 1944 when the decree came to deliver all the children in the Lodz ghetto to the Nazis—the precious children. We cared for them and tried*

4

to build a warm, secure, and loving environment. Now we had to deliver them to the Nazi murderers. There was no choice.

The next morning we had to bring them to a big stadium filled with German soldiers and trucks. Ironically, the loudspeakers were blasting with German children's songs. I was so torn with emotion. We all knew the destination of the children. In my arms I held six-year-old David, who was so stricken with meningitis. I had carried him on a pillow to ease his pain. Suddenly, the beast of a soldier tore the child from my arms and threw him on the truck.

I was screaming with all my heart, but didn't make a sound.

My mother's silence was rooted in fear and oppression—so different from the silence of indifference that helped perpetuate one of history's greatest human atrocities. From the Lodz ghetto, my mother was shipped from one concentration camp to another: Auschwitz-Birkenau, Stutthof, Thereisenstadt. When she first arrived in Auschwitz, she came with her best friend, Pola. My mother shares her story:

You should have seen me. My head was shaved; I was wearing wooden shoes, a flimsy dress, and no undergarments. I came with my dearest friend, Pola. We had to call out our names to recognize each other. It was the middle of winter. We were freezing and frightened.

One day, two soldiers were walking me to the train station. And I'll never forget, there were a bunch of German civilians who were reading the newspaper. They were going to work in the morning and I was looking desperately at their faces and thinking, "Let them see me. Let them see what they are doing." But they just buried their heads in the paper. I was invisible.

In Auschwitz, my mother bore witness to the unspeakable, while others closed their eyes. By the time she was liberated in May of 1945, she was the sole survivor of a family that had once numbered sixty-five.

Over the years, I have frequently asked my mother why she thinks she survived. She has shared with me that what motivated her to face each day of torture was her dream of one day getting married and having a husband and children. In the direst of times, she frequently fantasized about how her family had sat together at the holiday table, singing songs and enjoying traditional holiday foods. Then she thought about how wonderful it would be to one day have her own family celebrating together.

These fantasies gave her the hope and will to carry on. She also said that being with other people in the camps, even though many spoke different languages, helped sustain her. Had she been in isolation, it would have been much harder for her to survive. The group's collective strength supported her. The most important thing in my mother's life to this day is her family and being connected to people and sharing life's experiences with them.

Henry Greenspan

My father, Henry Greenspan, was born in Krakow, Poland on May 4, 1919. He had two younger brothers, Leon and Arthur. He attended the Hebrew *gymnasium* in Poland, a secondary school where he became fluent in Hebrew and well versed in Jewish studies. He also enjoyed skiing, horseback riding, and swimming. His parents, Nathan and Golda, were involved in many businesses, one of which was buying and selling corals.

When Hitler invaded Poland, their lives changed forever. My grandfather, father, and Uncle Leon were incarcerated in the Plaszow Concentration Camp in Krakow. My grandparents tried to save Arthur, who was only nine-years-old, by paying a Polish family to hide him until he obtained Hungarian papers and a passport. Young children and the elderly were the first to be killed by the Nazis because they were not able to work.

While in Plaszow, my father, uncle, and grandfather worked for Oskar Schindler in his factory called Emalia, where he produced enamel goods and munitions for the German army. Schindler would later become famous for employing and ultimately saving 1,200 of his Jewish employees by claiming that he couldn't keep his factory running without them. While they worked at Emalia, my family was protected, fed, and clothed. Unfortunately they were not on Schindler's famous "list," the subject of Steven Spielberg's film *Schindler's List*. They did not go to Brinnlitz, Czechoslovakia where Schindler relocated his factory; but instead were sent on the death march to Germany.

Toward the end of the war in 1944, the Nazis wanted to erase evidence of the concentration camps, and the atrocities committed in them. They forced the Jews to walk for hundreds of miles under extreme cold and harsh conditions. They were brutally mistreated by the SS guards, and went without food, water, or shelter. Anyone who could not keep up was killed instantly. Both my parents were on the death march, and were interned at the Thereisenstadt Concentration Camp outside Prague.

My parents met after the Russian army liberated the camp in May of 1945. Both were suffering from typhus and weighed eighty pounds each. They resided in separate male and female convalescent areas within the camp. My father liked to tell the story of how my parents met. One day, he went to the women's convalescent area, and saw my mother. He said to her, "If you could change your dress, and put on something nice, I would take you dancing." She replied, "This dress is made out of a tablecloth, but unfortunately, it is all that I have. So if you want to take me dancing, you'll have to take me as I am."

This was the beginning of their courtship. Once they were able to, they traveled to Krakow to see if they could find any surviving family members or friends. Miraculously, through a family friend, my father found his mother Golda and brother Leon. It was extraordinary that Leon was alive, but it was even more amazing that my grandmother had survived at age fifty. My grandfather Nathan had died in the concentration camp Mathausen. Arthur, tragically, was handed over to the Nazis by the family that was entrusted with his care.

7

My mother traveled to Lodz and found that her whole family of sixty-five people had been killed. She always tells me how grateful she was to meet my father, but the added bonus, she says, was that his mother and one of his brothers were still alive. They became an instant family that was inseparable. Being together took away some of my mother's pain and anguish after she discovered the magnitude of her own loss.

My father was smitten by my mother and immediately proposed. He told her that he was sorry that he could not give her a ring for their engagement. Upon hearing this, my grandmother shared with excitement that she, in fact, had a way to give my mother a ring. She said that before the war she had a premonition of doom, and had given her Sabbath candlesticks and one of her most valued coral stones to a Polish man who had worked for her in the family coral business. She had also provided him a place to live in a four-story building owned by her family, and asked him to watch over the building and these few precious belongings. My grandmother was very excited that she would be able to give these treasured items to my parents as a wedding gift.

My father went with my grandmother and found the man to whom she had entrusted her building and these possessions. He had moved into the building with many of his family members and friends. When he saw my father and grandmother, he became ashen and started shaking. He was afraid that they had come to take back the building. My grandmother assured him that she had no interest in the building because they did not plan to stay in Poland, but wanted him to return the coral stone and candlesticks.

In spite of the great losses they had endured, the man denied having these possessions. He firmly stated that he never had received the candlesticks or the coral stone. Exasperated and dejected, my grandmother and father went to the police and begged them to intercede. When the man realized that the police might become involved, he sheepishly handed over the items. Even though the war was over, this man was so filled with hate and greed that he had no compassion for their suffering and loss. My parents were astounded at his lack of humanity, but they would not let it detract from their joy in having found each other and their plans to marry, start a new life, and create a family.

A Coral Ring: A Symbol of Courage

My grandmother Golda's coral stone became the centerpiece of my mother's engagement ring. For my fiftieth birthday, my mother gave me this ring. Every time I look at my right hand and see it, I am reminded of my family history. This ring, which brought so much joy to my mother, is a daily reminder of the values that my family taught me. It is my most treasured possession.

As I reflect upon this ring, and what it means to me, it teaches me about the courage displayed by Holocaust survivors. Many times I have heard people question why the Jews went to the gas chambers "like sheep to slaughter," showing no resistance. On the contrary, my parents and the other survivors showed resistance by waking up each day to face their perpetrators and endless physical and emotional torture. Despite the unthinkable and horrific circumstances facing them, my family showed great character, and true courage. My mother tried to bring love and joy to the children whom she took care of in the orphanage in the Lodz ghetto. My father carried his cousin on his back when he was too weak to continue on the death march. Each time I see my cousin Henek, now ninety-years-old, he reminds me of his gratitude to my father for being so selfless.

When my grandmother was sent to Auschwitz, she found herself standing face to face with Dr. Josef Mengele, the "Angel of Death," who was directing people to the right and left, and in so doing, determining who would live and who would die. In that instant, she decided that no matter what Mengele told her, she would go to the line where the younger Jews were being directed. Despite Mengele's instructions, she quietly moved to the right, and thereby escaped the crematoria for the first time. She realized that further survival required that she looked as young and healthy as possible Using her knowledge of Italian, she befriended an Italian doctor in the camp, who had access to the infirmary where they stored purple cleaning crystals, which he gave to my grandmother. She used these crystals to make a black hair dye that she shared with others and exchanged for food. She also found berries growing in Auschwitz and used them to apply a red rouge-like substance to women's cheeks. The hair dye and berries made them appear healthier and able to work. Through these selfless actions, she helped save hundreds of lives. These were extraordinary acts of humanity performed under the worst of circumstances. This was true courage.

The Child of Survivors: A New Beginning in America

I grew up with these stories, and they have inspired me throughout my life. This was my heritage. But I couldn't let it rest there. I didn't want these atrocities to be my family's only legacy. I had to turn it around somehow for them. I had to try to give meaning to their senseless suffering and to model a message that we are responsible for one another—that as individuals, we can influence the human condition for good, knowing that it can just as easily be subjected to evil.

My parents, grandmother, and I came to the United States when I was three-years-old. We didn't speak a word of English, and my family had no money or formal professional training. We settled in New York City, in the Washington Heights area of Manhattan, joined by hundreds of other Holocaust survivors. I went to *yeshiva*, a Jewish day school, because my parents wanted me to become educated in Jewish studies. In spite of what happened to them, they never lost their belief in God. They felt that because they had been singled out by the Nazis for the crime of being born Jewish, their responsibility was to imbue their love of Judaism in their children.

The yeshiva's curriculum was quite rigorous. We spent half of each day studying Hebrew language, Hebrew literature, laws and customs, the Bible, and Talmud. The other half of the day was devoted to English, math, science, social studies, music, and art. I got home at 5:00 PM and had at least three-to-four hours of homework each night. My mother told me that although she understood this school was very demanding, she felt it would give me the background to succeed in life. There were many times I resented not having more time to play, but I liked my friends at school and enjoyed mastering so many different subjects. College and graduate school seemed relatively easy compared to my early education.

My mother always revered education and went to night school to learn English. She learned to crochet, and worked making dresses and evening gowns to help supplement my father's modest income. She became very talented at this craft, but eventually had to give it up when her eyesight began to suffer from the intricate work. Her life was very busy because in addition to working and taking care of our family, we had taken in two boarders for whom she cooked and cleaned to help to make ends meet.

My mother has always been my best friend and closest advisor. Even though her life's dreams were cut short when Hitler invaded Poland, she always had dreams for me and my brother, Josh. She inspired us to become whatever we wanted to be and told us to *dream big*.

From my father I learned to be tenacious. When he first arrived in the United States, he worked in a pickle factory in Manhattan. He was very unhappy with this job and struggled to make a living. His brother Leon had relocated to Canada, and became involved in Toronto's burgeoning furniture business. Every summer, my grandmother, my parents, and I traveled to Toronto and spent several weeks at Lake Simcoe with a group of Holocaust survivors, including my Uncle Leon and his wife Barbara. Eventually, my parents decided that we should move to Toronto so that my father could go into the furniture business with my uncle, a gifted and resourceful businessman.

In 1956, my mother became pregnant, and so there was an even greater urgency to make money. My aunt and uncle had two children, seventeen-month-old Norman and two-month-old Mark. There was an excitement about reuniting the family, and creating a family business that could comfortably support us all.

I was eight-years-old in 1956, and vividly remember coming home from school one day and seeing my parents and grandmother crying hysterically. I had never witnessed anything like this in my young life. They asked me to be quiet and would not tell me why they were crying. My parents were speaking in Polish and Yiddish, which I did not really understand, but I was able to begin to piece the story together.

My Uncle Leon had gone to one of his furniture stores, and unknown to him, an elevator had malfunctioned. He stepped into an empty elevator shaft and fell to his death. My family was devastated. We never moved to Canada, but instead went to his funeral. For my grandmother to have lost yet another son after what she had experienced was unfathomable. It was a very painful time for our family. How much suffering could they bear? Once again, my parents, grandmother, and relatives in Toronto displayed great strength and courage. My brother was born in March of that year. Slowly, my family began to pull themselves out of their grief, as there were children to love and care for.

Times were tough for my family. My parents and grandmother had few possessions, and they spent what little they did have to buy things for my brother and me. One day, a survivor friend whom my father had known from Poland, asked my father to work with him in the textile business. He taught my father the trade, and over the years my father was able to make a good living in this business.

As I got older, my father shared with me his formula for success. He would go from building-to-building, floor-to-floor in the garment center, selling his fabrics. If someone rejected him, he became even more determined, and would go from business to business. He had many difficult days, but eventually there were also profitable days. He taught me never to give up and to try harder when you are rejected. These lessons have helped me deal more effectively with problems I have encountered in my own life.

My Parents Taught Me Well

The most important value that my mother taught me was to be a *mensch*. Lest the term lose any of its meaning in translation, consider the words of Rabbi Neil Kurshan in his book *Raising Your Child to Be a Mensch*:

> *The term "mensch" literally means … "person"…but it represents a moral ideal for all people, men and women alike… It means being sensitive to other people's needs and seeking out ways to help them. It is acquired by living close*

> *to family and extending one's sense of obligation beyond*
> *the family to the broader community. In the Jewish culture*
> *of Eastern Europe where the term arose, to call someone a*
> mensch *was the highest compliment that could be given.*

When my brother and I strove for academic success, our mother was there to keep us on track. And she wasn't subtle. "Go. Do well in school. But first and foremost, be a *mensch!* Then you can do anything." I'd bring home a perfect test score and she'd say, "Yes, but were you a *mensch* today?" At the time I didn't understand why she put so much emphasis on this. I do now.

My brother and I and our friends, who were also children of survivors, all felt that we had to become what author Helen Epstein classified as "nachas machines" in her book *Children of the Holocaust.* It meant dispensing joy to make our parents happy—to try to take away their pain and suffering. We all worked hard to get good grades, tried not to get in trouble, made good choices, and were accepted to good colleges.

However, part of assuaging our parents' fears for our safety also meant making personal sacrifices. For me, this meant never learning how to ride a bike or roller-skate, or become involved in any sport or activity that could potentially hurt me. I was being raised to be the perfect couch potato. My mother always said that she could not bear to see me get hurt, and sheltered me from all these activities. It was not until I was in my twenties and had children of my own that I attempted to learn to ride a bike.

Oma Golda: A Powerful Role Model

When I was a young girl, I shared a bedroom with my grandmother Golda, whom I called "Oma." Oma was a woman who was always ahead of her time. She was determined, ambitious, hard working, and capable. She truly epitomized the survivor. She never complained about the tragedies of her life or about her health, and she was grateful for each day that she shared with us. Oma was an inspiration to me. As a young child, I was mesmerized by her stories of how in the early 1900s, at age fifteen, she had traveled from Krakow, Poland to Livorno, Italy to help with the family's coral business. She taught me that women can do anything that we put our minds to. Oma was a real entrepreneur and a powerful role model.

Every morning, she would walk me to the school bus, and in the evening she would pick me up. She encouraged me to do well in school and insisted that I go to bed early and wake up at 5:00 AM to study. She told me that when she was young, she would get up early to learn Italian, a language she remembered to the very end. The day before she died at the age of ninety-six, she recited passages from *Dante's Inferno* in Italian, and then translated them into Yiddish and English. She was a very hard-working woman who instilled in my brother and me a need to succeed. In German she would say, "Kop Hoch," which means "keep your head high." That was her motto.

Oma told me that to maintain her courage and humanity while she was in the concentration camps, she would repeatedly tell herself that she was still *Golda Greenspan* and *not* the number that the Nazis tattooed to her forearm to identify her. By maintaining her individuality, she was able to also maintain her dignity, sanity, and will to live. This was her personal protest against the Nazi's dehumanizing act of taking away their victims' names and identities.

From my parents and my grandmother, I learned to never give up—especially when things are difficult. They told me that women, like men, can be successful and do whatever they put their minds to. In the 1950s and 1960s, that was very progressive thinking. They were positive and wanted their children to have the best lives possible, despite what they themselves had been through.

Lives of Joy and Giving

My family was very charitable. They taught me to always help others. Anytime that there was a collection for someone in need, my father always gave, regardless of how little money we had. Indeed, he was often the one who organized the collection. From him I learned firsthand that helping others is a responsibility and a privilege. After the war, my father and many of his survivor friends showed their loyalty and gratitude to Oskar Schindler. They sent him money and gifts, and flew him to the United States for family celebrations of marriages and births. Giving charity and caring for others was the key to being a *mensch*.

For many years, my parents were part of a group of survivors from Krakow who formed the New Krakow Friendship Society to stay connected, share information through newsletters and meetings, and raise money for philanthropic causes. Over the years, they have donated funds for ambulances, equipment for rehabilitation units, and hospital buildings, and given money to families in need in the United States and in Israel. This group frequently traveled to Israel to meet other survivors and visit the many institutions they helped support. They were the core of my parents' social life.

Once my father started earning a comfortable living, my family joined their Holocaust survivor friends each summer in bungalow colonies in the Catskill Mountains in New York State. These survivors became my extended family. I quickly learned how vital and powerful their friendships were. They supported one another through difficult times and shared in one another's joy in good times. Despite enduring the worst of humanity, they came together to celebrate life. They would sit in their lounge chairs outside their bungalows and reminisce about what had happened to them, and then focus on the gifts that they had: their children and grandchildren. Through their deeds, these family friends taught me so much about life and how to live it to the fullest.

Every Saturday night, they dressed in their finest clothes, hired a musician to play the piano, and danced into the wee hours of the morning. They loved to tell jokes. For me, they modeled that life is a gift to be enjoyed and not to be taken for granted. As a young girl, I remember admiring how beautiful my mother looked as she dressed for the evening's party. Her smile was always radiant, and appeared lifetimes away from the terror and loss that once consumed her. She taught me to always look my best and treasure what I have—to live in the moment. I understood from an early age that in spite of what had happened to my parents, they cherished their lives and did their best to live with great joy.

These summers were the happiest times of my childhood. My parents continued to go to the Catskills every summer well into their eighties.

The Core Lessons

Growing up, I heard several Hebrew and Yiddish phrases that my parents used when they discussed the Holocaust. They felt that these words captured the essence of their Holocaust legacy:

- Zachor (*Hebrew*)/ Gedenk (*Yiddish*): Remember.
- Fargess nicht (*Yiddish*): Never forget.

When I asked them what the difference was between remembering and never forgetting, I was told that remembering was reflecting on the events that happened during the Holocaust and memorializing the victims. It was about remembering the names and stories of the many relatives whose pictures I had never seen and whom I had never met. It was about remembering the stories my parents told me about their horrific experiences, as well as their beautiful lives before the war.

My parents explained that besides remembering, I must also never forget. They explained that they pledged to each other in the camps that if they survived they would never forget those who perished. "To never forget" means that we must move beyond commemoration and be *proactive*. To do something to ensure that atrocities of this magnitude never again happen to anyone.

These were the values that my parents instilled in me from a young age. Instead of being bitter and angry about what had happened to them, they chose to teach my brother and me to love, show compassion for others, and to stand up for what is right. They stressed that because they had miraculously survived, that we, as a family, needed to live our legacy and make the world a better place.

My parents expanded on this by teaching me these seven important lessons:

1. Silence and indifference are diseases that must be combated.
2. We must always stand up and speak up for what we believe.
3. The greatest gift we have in our lives is freedom.
4. We must teach character and compassion.
5. A head without a heart is dangerous.
6. We must be proud of who we are and be true to ourselves and our convictions.
7. It is everyone's responsibility and privilege to make the world a better place.

As a child and teenager, any setback I suffered paled in comparison to my parents' experiences. How could it not? How could I compare a snub at the playground, or a poor test score, or the lack of a prom date to the inhumanity of Auschwitz? Whenever I faced a challenge or was overcome with self-doubt, my mother in particular would remind me that I had the power to do anything. She would say, "There's the moon and the sun, and they both shine. But the sun also warms, and you are the sun." Her words resounded loud and clear in my head when I faced some of life's difficulties and disappointments. They gave me perspective on what is truly important. They taught me the skills that gave me the inner strength I needed to approach challenges with poise and purpose.

These lessons have stayed with me all my life. I have taught them to my children and grandchildren. These lessons are the core of my organization, Champions of Caring.

CHAPTER 1 GUIDING QUESTIONS

- What is the meaning of your name? What does this name mean to you? To others?
- What is your family history? What lessons have you learned from this history?
- Have you or your family suffered prejudice, hatred, or tragedy?
- How did you or they react?
- What did they learn from this experience?
- What did you learn from this experience?
- Do you have a special family heirloom?
- What does it mean to you?
- What are the core teachings of your family?
- Are there any incidents in your youth that influenced the direction of your life?
- What role did parents, grandparents, or other family members play in your life?

Chapter 2. CONFRONTING MY LEGACY

Milestones

As I grew older and recognized how the lessons that I learned from my parents influenced my life, I wanted to share them with others. My mother's love for children was contagious and she inspired me to go into teaching. I was the first person in my family to go to college.

The process of selecting a college for me was quite interesting. My parents had several criteria: Was it a good school? Was it in a safe neighborhood? How much did it cost to attend? How far was it from our apartment? How many trains or buses would I need to take? After much deliberation and discussion, we chose Hunter College in the Bronx (now called Lehman College). They knew it was part of the City University System of New York, which had a fine reputation. It was in an area in the Bronx that was safe and familiar to my parents. I only needed to take two buses to get there, and best of all, tuition was *$39 a semester*. I was happy with this choice because several of my friends were going there.

However, my father became very unhappy when he heard that after paying the tuition, he still had to pay for books. I remember coming home with my used books, which had been marked up with pen and highlighter, and seeing how appalled my father was that anyone would have the audacity to write in a book. He was furious that the school had the *chutzpah* to charge money for a book in this condition. Thirty years later, I was honored by being inducted into the Hunter College Hall of Fame. As part of my acceptance speech, I shared these stories. My father sat in the front row with a proud smile on his face.

Because I lived at home, I was able share with my mother what I learned in my college classes, and we became closer than ever. It was a joyous opportunity for us to learn together, and even more invaluable for me to hear her insights about my studies. Although her formal education was put to an abrupt end at age twenty, her life experiences and perspectives on people, issues, and humanity were powerful. What she taught me was so much more valuable than anything I ever learned from a textbook. I remember my mother was once asked by a reporter if she had gone to college. She immediately responded, "Oh yes, I went to a very unique college where I learned more about humanity, morality, and life than one could ever imagine. I was in Auschwitz and what I saw and experienced there can never be taught in a classroom."

While my education was very important me, so was creating a family life. On December 24th, 1967, one month shy of my twentieth birthday, I married my first husband, Michael Eisenbud. I had met Mike six months before at a party at Columbia University, where he was attending the graduate business school. My wedding was a very moving event. My parents had invited close to 300 people to witness this joyous occasion. It was one of the first weddings of my generation that the survivors had attended. The awe and excitement of the evening was palpable. The survivors came running up to me and Mike, and were crying with joy, saying "I was in Auschwitz with your mother. I cannot believe we lived to see this day," and "I grew up with your father in Krakow. This is a miracle!" For my parents and their group of friends, witnessing this milestone was almost incomprehensible. Who would have ever thought *they* could have married and had children, let alone marry off a daughter?

At the time of my marriage, I was a junior in college and I still needed twelve credits to graduate. Mike had completed his MBA and was recruited by General Electric for a job in Daytona Beach, Florida. As a new bride, I was conflicted because I so badly wanted to go with him to Florida, but I knew I had to finish college. It was my mother who advised me to live at home that summer and finish my degree. She convinced my father to pay for me to visit Mike twice over the summer months. I finally agreed, even though it went against my wishes. My mother had the vision and foresight to ensure that I completed my education.

A Head without a Heart Is Dangerous

After completing my degree, I joined Mike in Daytona Beach, where I experienced my first episodes of anti-Semitism. During an interview for a teaching position, the interviewer asked, "What kind of a name is Eisenbud?" Not fully understanding the meaning of this question, I quickly and nervously responded, "American." "No, no," he said, "What's your religion?" This made me terribly uncomfortable, but he continued with this line of questioning. "You're Jewish! I have the perfect school for you. You'll love it. You'll fit right in." He was half right. I did love my new school. But I didn't exactly fit in. I soon realized that I was the only white teacher in a segregated elementary school.

I loved my thirty-three first graders. It was a challenge and a joy to teach them. I wanted to give them new opportunities and experiences. I took them swimming at the pool in my apartment complex. Florida was highly segregated in the 1960s and my white neighbors were up in arms. But this did not deter me. I also was in charge of arranging our staff holiday party. I'll never forget the looks on the faces of the other patrons at the very upscale restaurant we went to when I showed up for the party with thirty-five black teachers. This was my personal protest. Because of my own family history and experiences with prejudice, it was painful for me to witness how prejudiced people were against African Americans. It strengthened my resolve to become a change agent and speak up to improve education, because I knew in my heart (as well as in the law) that separate could never be equal.

While at this school, I encountered a truly bizarre incident of ignorance and prejudice. One day, an itinerant white music teacher, Edwina, came to our school. We had instant chemistry and became friendly. Edwina was originally from Macon, Georgia. She was in her twenties and had just completed her master's degree in education. She started coming to the school to teach every few weeks. One day she came to school and realized that I was absent. I had taken the day off for a Jewish holy day. When Edwina saw me the following week, she told me that she was concerned that I had not been there and asked if I was all right. I explained that I had taken time off to celebrate Passover. Edwina instantly got a strange look on her face, then raised her arms and passed her hands back and forth over my head. I was puzzled by the action. Stupefied, I asked her what she was doing. Her reply was shocking: "Looking for your horns."

She went on to explain that her father had taught her that all Jews were evil, and had horns like the devil. I couldn't believe what was happening. How could an educated woman believe this? And how could she in turn be an *educator*? Why did her father hate Jews—especially since she told me that he had never met one in Macon? From that day on, Edwina avoided me. I started to dislike living in Florida. The evils of segregation that I had observed, and my own experiences of anti-Semitism, upset me terribly. I committed myself to finding a way to educate others so that this type of hatred, which had caused my family so much suffering, would not be repeated.

Telling My Story

In 1970, Mike and I moved from Daytona to Pittsfield, Massachusetts. I was teaching kindergarten in Pittsfield when I learned that John Crystal, who co-authored the book *What Color Is Your Parachute?* (with Richard Nelson Bolles), was offering a workshop for teachers to help them identify their skills and empower them to be successful. I was interested in being part of this workshop, but was initially reluctant to join. First, it was costly to attend, and I didn't know where I would get the money. Second, every participant had to submit a fifty-page autobiography, and the thought of putting my life down on paper was stressful. When I told my mother about the course, she offered to give me the money because she believed that this was something that I needed to do. Her mantra was, "Bella, be independent, get the best schooling, make your own money, and always stand on your own two feet. You never know where life takes you." I eventually took her advice and signed up for the course. This was one of the best decisions I ever made.

I struggled with writing my autobiography. Every time I tried to put to paper the story of my life and my parents' experiences, I broke down in tears, and stopped writing. I didn't want to write from a sad or weak perspective. Finally, I pulled an all-nighter, and wrote nonstop. I reflected on my parents' history, and how it taught me to be strong and to have dreams and high aspirations. I wrote about how their experiences shaped my views and influenced my decision to become a teacher.

I submitted my assignment and attended the workshop. Over the course of the sessions, John Crystal used the activities from his book to help us assess our skills; what we liked and disliked about our jobs; the environments we felt comfortable working in; and the types of opportunities we secretly wanted to pursue. I was very taken by what he was teaching, and it changed my outlook on my future.

One day, John asked me to stay after the session. He shared with me that he had read my story, and was very moved. Then he started to get teary-eyed, and I wasn't sure why. He told me that he had been in a U.S. army unit that helped liberate the concentration camps. He explained that this experience had changed his life, and when he read what I had written, it brought back those memories. Having witnessed the horrors of the Holocaust firsthand, he was moved by the strength of my conviction and my desire to do good work. He told me that I had great potential, and should stay open to new possibilities. He said, "I know that one day you'll change the world for the better." At age twenty-two, that statement was hard for me to believe, or understand.

Aside from my parents and grandmother, John had one of the biggest impacts on my life regarding how I thought about my career path, and what I wanted to accomplish. His workshop really opened my mind to the idea that even though I was trained to be a teacher, I had skills that could be adapted to new challenges. For me, that was a novel concept in 1970. Although my mother had told me to dream big, I didn't think that women had many career choices. In those days, my girlfriends and I felt that we could only be teachers, nurses or secretaries. It never dawned on me that any other professions were available to me. John helped me to recognize that, in fact, there were a host of other possibilities that I could pursue. I stayed in touch with him after that workshop, and contacted him whenever I made career moves. Sadly, he passed away, but I think of him frequently, and will always be grateful to him for teaching me to have faith in myself and welcome new and challenging opportunities.

What I learned from John also empowered me to get involved in the women's movement. I began running seminars and workshops teaching women to identify their skills and interests, write resumes that better represented their accomplishments, and master interviewing techniques. I wanted to motivate them to have confidence in themselves and be able to compete for better jobs.

My Mother Finds Her Voice

My experience in writing my autobiography motivated me to want to share my family's history with others. In 1971, I persuaded my mother to tell her story publicly at a United Jewish Appeal meeting in Pittsfield. It is indescribable how painful it was for my mother to recount the horrific details of her time in the death camps. I wanted to shield her from any more suffering, and she wanted to protect me from the torture she and my father had endured. Yet we both knew that it was important to get her message out to others. It was a huge psychological and emotional risk for my mother and me, but ultimately worthwhile to face our own pain so that people could learn that these horrific events can and do occur when we close our eyes, ears, and hearts to humanity.

This was the first of many speaking engagements that my mother and I would organize in an effort to create awareness about her experiences during the Holocaust. At that time, few survivors had come forward. Indeed, many had been encouraged by fellow survivors, friends and relatives *not* to speak about their experiences. Having been singled out so brutally in the not-so-distant past, they were reluctant to call attention to themselves. Gradually, as the years passed, the movement to publicly address the anguish they had experienced grew stronger.

For many years, my mother spoke to students in schools in Harlem and the Bronx about her experiences during the Holocaust. After she spoke, students would frequently approach her and thank her for having the courage to share these experiences. In return, they would share their own pain with her. Some even confided that they were suicidal, that life was just too difficult for them. To give them strength, she told them, "The sun came out for me after Auschwitz. It will come out for you as well. You must trust and believe in yourself." Many of these young people have written my mother letters of gratitude for inspiring them to go on, even though they had hardships in their lives.

My mother and one of her survivor friends started a Holocaust group in Riverdale, a suburb of the Bronx, to bring together local survivors to share their stories and raise awareness about current injustices and genocide. She has spent the last thirty years, until she became too ill, giving interviews and speeches, and writing articles to combat Holocaust denial and revisionism. Sharing the lessons of the Holocaust has been her life's mission, and it also became mine.

Educating Students' Hearts and Minds

While living in Pittsfield, I had the challenge of working with Title I high school students who could not read, write, or do math at grade level. Title I is a program created by the U.S. Department of Education that provides extra help to failing students from low-income families. Many of my students had been in trouble with the law.

I was given the task of creating a program that would motivate them to take school more seriously and help them become successful in life. I developed a work readiness program and worked with community partners, including the hospital, mayor's office, and corporations, to organize on-site visits for these students so they could learn more about their community and potential job opportunities that would be available to them after graduation. Typically, the students met with supervisors who explained the benefits of working at their company, the importance of having a good work ethic, and shared with the students that they would be available to help them get entry-level jobs. The kids would leave these meetings feeling positive and hopeful about the possibility of having a better life.

After several of these outings, I remember bringing the students back to the high school and being admonished by the principal for keeping them out too long. That day, the bus was very late picking us up and they missed their English class, which was covering *Romeo and Juliet*. Many of the students had told me that they cut this class with regularity because they felt it had no meaning in their lives. The principal was livid and yelled at me in front of the students.

Upon reflection, I realized that I had reached a point where my efforts to be creative and motivate these students to succeed, and stay out of trouble, were not appreciated, and even disparaged. I wanted to educate their hearts as well as their minds, and give them hope for a better future, but my approach was not supported by the administration. It was then that I lost my enthusiasm to work in education under this type of system.

I turned my career in another direction, but always missed working with youth and hoped that one day I could return to the field. Isn't it interesting that thirty years later, I am once again following my passion, working with youth *and* being more creative than ever?

Motherhood

My husband's position with General Electric caused us to move to a new location every three years. This was a challenge because I had to keep reinventing myself. Throughout all of these reinventions, however, my most fulfilling role was motherhood. When my children Deborah and Daniel were born, I stopped working and became a stay-at-home mom. The time with them was precious. The miracle of having and raising my own children was the most joyous time of my life. To be twenty-three years old and have children was the greatest gift I could ever imagine. I wanted to savor every moment. I knew that the first five years of a child's life were the most formative, and I wanted to be there for each milestone. I learned with my children how to ski, play tennis, and even ride a bike. It was my own second childhood, but I never told my mother about my athletic achievements. She would not have been happy …

I wanted to shelter my children from my family's painful history, but realized, when appropriate, they needed to learn those invaluable lessons. My mother, whom they call *Savtah*, was an extraordinary grandmother and always knew what to share with them about her life's experiences.

I am very proud of my children and all of their accomplishments, but what I am *most* proud of is how they continue to live our family legacy. My son Dan is a successful magazine editor and a wonderful writer. He has written extraordinary testimonials about my mother and what he has learned from her experiences. He shared the following at her eighty-sixth birthday:

> *I'm no prince, but one thing's for sure: I'm the descendent of royalty. Not the kind of arbitrary royalty that comes from luck and a name—but earned nobility.*
>
> *To say that my grandmother is a wonderful person is like saying that flowers and babies are beautiful. It's a given. Carola Greenspan is a brilliant, forgiving ray of light in a world that can be cruel and dark.*
>
> *If you ever feel beaten by life—like you just can't fathom how you're going to make it through the day—you just visit my grandmother, hold her hand, and look into her eyes for a good few seconds. I promise that if you do this you will see a strength so profound and majestic that you will be able to carry on knowing that there is meaning where you once saw none.*

Not a Saturday goes by that he does not visit her, bringing love and beautiful roses.

My daughter Deb is an assistant district attorney prosecuting criminals and bringing them to justice. She also worked at Champions of Caring, helping me design new programs and write grant applications. She and her husband Jeremy are teaching their children Jacob and Rebecca the importance of good character and standing up and speaking out for what they believe in. I was blessed to be in the delivery room for my grandchildren's births. The first thing I said to them as I held them with tears of joy in my eyes was "You will be a *mensch*. You will be a Champion." To be able to teach these lessons to yet another generation is truly a privilege.

Reinventing Myself, Yet Again

When Deb and Dan were seven and six, respectively, I felt I could move beyond the home again. I taught Hebrew school two afternoons a week and worked on getting my master's degree in education. I tried to balance the needs of my husband and children, and my desire to improve myself. I also began volunteering and became involved with Holocaust commemoration activities in the community, the United Jewish Appeal, and planning adult education seminars.

In 1979, we left Pittsfield and moved to Syracuse, New York, where I got a job marketing *Häagen-Dazs®* ice cream, which was then a new brand. I loved creating marketing plans and meeting clients—and particularly enjoyed the challenge of convincing restaurants, hospitals and universities why they should buy a product they could barely pronounce (and thought I made in my basement).

At the time, I was also active with the Chemical People Project, a program to fight drug and alcohol abuse among teens. I enjoyed working with politicians, educators and corporate leaders to educate the community about the importance of staying drug-free. I also served on the board of directors for my synagogue and chaired a committee to address the special needs of our congregants. I always tried to model for my children that they could be whatever they wanted to be, but that it was important to always give back.

In 1984, we moved yet again from Syracuse to Philadelphia, and I became a consultant and then a partner at an executive search firm, recruiting senior-level health care executives and physicians. I heard John Crystal's words echoing in my ears, "You can sell concepts, products, or ideas. If the opportunity is there, embrace it."

In 1987, with fear and trepidation, I founded my own search firm, Eisenbud & Associates. We recruited for health-care institutions all over the United States. This was a very gutsy and challenging undertaking, but it taught me a great deal. I felt very proud to be a woman running my own company. It never dawned on me while growing up in the 1950s and 1960s, that this was even possible.

My professional life was challenging, but it was balanced by active involvement within the community. At that time, I was the chair of the Memorial Committee of the Six Million Jewish Martyrs for the Jewish Community Relations Council of Greater Philadelphia, working on programs to educate the community about the lessons of the Holocaust. I was also on the board of the Southeastern Pennsylvania chapter of the American Red Cross and the Hebrew Immigrant Aid Society (HIAS). This gave me great pleasure and added meaning to my life. I loved my work, but something was still missing. I needed to do more, but wasn't sure *what*.

Facing the Horrors of the Holocaust

In 1985, my parents, my brother, and I attended the World Gathering of Jewish Holocaust Survivors in Philadelphia. Josh and I were both very dedicated to our parents, and frequently attended conferences with them. One afternoon, an entire assemblage of survivors and their children marched to the Liberty Bell. As we linked arm-in-arm, my mother said, without hesitation, "I want to go back to Poland, and I want to show everyone that Hitler did not succeed with his 'Final Solution.' We are alive. We are well. We have made wonderful lives for ourselves. We have children and are proud Americans and Jews." Although we were stunned by her request, we felt that we had to honor it.

In 1989, my parents, my brother, and I traveled to Poland with one-hundred Holocaust survivors and their families. My brother, who is a physician, packed a variety of medications fearing how the trip may impact our parents physically and emotionally. Ironically, he and I were the ones who would end up taking the medications.

The trip was powerful and changed me forever. The day we went to Auschwitz was excruciatingly painful. In anticipation, I worried about every detail; What does one even wear to Auschwitz? Black for mourning? White for rebirth? My mother, as always, had the answer. "You wear your Jewish pride and dignity," she said.

When my brother and I were young, my mother had a habit that irritated us. She compulsively brushed her teeth. We were always late because my mother had to brush her teeth, yet again. When I got to Auschwitz, I finally understood why. The Nazis had collected items that they confiscated from their victims in the camps. There were piles of eyeglasses, shoes, suitcases, and clothing displayed. We passed through each of these rooms, and finally arrived in a room filled with thousands of toothbrushes. My mother quietly turned to me and said, "All I had when I got to Auschwitz was my toothbrush, and they even took that away from me." A toothbrush: the remaining symbol of her humanity. I was so sickened by this image that I ran from the room into the courtyard.

Auschwitz is now a museum and is often the site of school trips. All types of souvenir items are sold at the museum store, which creates an atmosphere that belies the significance of the place. I saw a group of German teens, one of whom had a swastika shaved in his head, eating candy and clowning around. I was so shocked by their behavior that I yelled at them in German. I was appalled that even at Auschwitz there was no respect or decorum.

The Sabbath after our trip to Auschwitz, we went to the Ramu synagogue in Krakow, where my father was Bar Mitzvahed over sixty years before. He was honored that day to be called up to recite a blessing before the reading of the Torah. I had a glimpse of his life before the war and realized how vital the Jewish community had been. But even this event was almost ruined. While walking from the synagogue to our hotel, we saw an old Polish man with a young boy. He pointed at our group and said in Polish *"Zid, zid, zid."* "A Jew, a Jew, a Jew." So many years later, and after unthinkable atrocities, this man was *still* teaching hate and contempt to an innocent child.

Seeing the room full of toothbrushes at Auschwitz, observing the lack of respect displayed by the boys who were visiting the camp, and witnessing the hatred that was being taught by a Polish man to a young child, made a huge impact on me. It angered me and further pushed me to want to do something to combat this type of behavior. But there was to be one last event on this trip that deeply moved me.

While in Krakow, my parents celebrated their wedding anniversary. It was very poignant because they were married there forty-eight years earlier. The members of the Krakow Jewish Community Center invited our group of survivors and their families for a luncheon celebration in honor of my parents' anniversary. Although the meal was quite modest, the love and caring that went into organizing this celebration were really extraordinary given that the people were old, quite frail, and of limited means.

At one point, the head of the Jewish community, Mrs. Jacubowicz, thanked us for coming and asked if it was possible for us to make a contribution to help those in dire need. I will never forget what she said: "Today I am in a position where I need to ask you for charity. It would be my dream to be privileged to give charity. One day, I hope I am in this luxurious position." These words profoundly touched me, and once again taught me that giving to others is truly a luxury and a *privilege.*

This encounter further strengthened my resolve to go back home and make a difference with my life. I realized how fortunate I was that I didn't need charity, and that I was in a position to help others.

Returning and Reflecting

Flying home to Philadelphia, I was choked with emotion and could not stop reflecting upon this trip, and my parents' tragic history. Growing up, my father used to say to me, "You will never understand what happened to us during the Holocaust." Finally, after witnessing the horrors of Auschwitz, as well as gaining a better understanding about the beautiful lives stolen from my parents, things became somewhat clearer. Although I can never truly comprehend how an evil of the magnitude of the Holocaust could ever happen, it is just as perplexing to me how the world could stand by, silent and indifferent. I realized on the trip that my family members were role models and heroes. If they had the strength and courage to comfort and save others during this horrific time, then certainly, I needed to take a stand and make a difference. I had to find my own way. This was all part of my legacy, and I needed to embrace it and live it *now*.

I returned to Philadelphia and knew I had to be proactive and educate others about the evils of prejudice and hatred. I had to make others aware of how the path of hate can lead to genocide. For years, I had told the story of my family. But now, I knew that I must do something more—not just *tell* the story, but *teach* its lessons. This trip changed me forever. I had to do something, but what? I wasn't quite sure.

And then Steven Spielberg released the film *Schindler's List* ...

CHAPTER 2 GUIDING QUESTIONS

- What were some of the tough decisions that you had to make at a young age? How did they impact your life?
- Have you had mentors? Who were they? How did they influence you and your life choices?
- Have you found your voice? Can you share your views and beliefs comfortably with others?
- What projects or programs have you been involved with, or created, that you are proud of?
- How did you respond when you failed or were criticized?
- Have you had to reinvent yourself professionally? What did you do?
- Have you volunteered in the past? For what?
- Have you pushed yourself to grow professionally? How and when?
- If you are a parent or grandparent, describe what makes your bond with your children or grandchildren special.
- If you are an aunt or uncle, do you have a special bond with your nieces and nephews? What makes your bond special?
- What are your core values in the workplace? Do they match up with your employer's values?
- Do you feel that something is missing in your life, or that you need more fulfillment?
- Have you had a life-changing event? How did it impact you?
- What did your parents or family teach you about character and respect?

Chapter 3. LIVING MY LEGACY

Close Encounter: A Meeting with Steven Spielberg

After returning home, I was haunted by my trip to Poland. When Spielberg released *Schindler's List,* I felt that this was karma. I was encouraged by my dear friends Bob and Suzanne Wright, whom I have known for the past thirty-five years, to write to Spielberg and thank him for making the film. Bob and Suzanne are the co-founders of Autism Speaks, and at the time of my letter, Bob was the CEO and chairman of NBC and Universal Studios. I had known the Wrights since my early married days when both my husband Michael and Bob were starting out with GE.

I wrote Spielberg that because of his film's power and international reach, he had done more to sensitize and educate people about the Holocaust than any historian or speaker ever could. I also took the opportunity to share with him my activities in Philadelphia and the work I had done to teach the lessons of the Holocaust to youth through my various volunteer positions. I explained that my passion was working with young people, and that I wanted to educate them about the importance of showing compassion, and giving back to their communities. In response, he wrote a personal letter of thanks, both for my words and for my efforts. This exchange prompted me to want to do even more to teach young people the lessons that I had learned from my parents.

A few months later, I learned that Spielberg would be at the Waldolf-Astoria Hotel in New York to receive a humanitarian award from Holocaust survivor and Nobel Prize winner, Elie Wiesel. My parents were invited, as were many "Schindler Jews." I decided that I had to go, too. I had to meet this man. Some opportunities present themselves; others are seized. This was a combination. While strolling through the Waldorf, I stumbled upon a private party. I had heard that Spielberg would be there, so, for lack of a more elegant term, I crashed. As I attempted to blend in, he arrived. No one noticed, so I advanced.

"Mr. Spielberg," I said, rushing to claim my moment. "My name is Barbara Eisenbud. I live in Philadelphia and I wrote you …"

"Stop," he said. "I know exactly who you are. I read your letter. I was very moved by your passion." He continued, "In about two minutes, the press is going to figure out that I've lost them, so I want to say a few things to you. I am very touched by your commitment. I would like to see you do something for kids. If you want to make a difference, inspire them to make the world better. Encourage them to do good work to repair the world. And then celebrate them as the heroes of our time."

His next words were magic. *"If you can do that, I will help you."*

That was the entire exchange. Thirty seconds? A minute at most. But that was all I needed. I thought to myself, "If I have his sponsorship, if I can prove to him that I'm worthy of his backing, this could turn into something extraordinary."

I don't remember actually driving back to Philadelphia. I was completely consumed by my close encounter with Steven Spielberg. Ideas raced through my mind, alternating between the analytical and the fantastic. He had said "heroes," and I thought: who are *heroes*? To me, they were the champions of truth and courage. How are great young people usually identified? Frequently, it's the student who gets straight A's, or the student with great athletic or musical talent. And I thought, hmmm. That's not what my parents taught me. I had learned about the *mensch* as the champion: the kid who goes out there and does something, not for glory, but because it's the *right thing to do*. I had read about teens who cared for the homeless, who visited people at hospices, who spent Thanksgiving at soup kitchens instead of football games, who bought teddy bears for young fire victims, who were really showing their humanity—but these weren't usually the stories we saw on television. We weren't reading or hearing enough about *these kids*. There it was! I had found it. My role would be to elevate young people who do great things—to celebrate them and publicize them as the heroes of our time. It resonated with me. These are the real heroes, the Champions of Caring.

Creating Champions of Caring: One Door Closes, Another Door Opens

I knew that my passion was working with youth. My mission would be to educate and empower them to be successful leaders. To teach them the skills to become social entrepreneurs—people who use their skills not to make money, but to improve the world. Then, I would take it one step further and tell the world about them to inspire others.

I was excited and driven to truly make a difference, but life is not always easy. At this time, my marriage of twenty five years was ending. It was a very painful and traumatic period for me. My children were in college, and for the first time in my life I found myself living alone. I had gone from my parents' home to living with my husband and my children. Now it was just me and my Wheaten Terrier, Barney. He became my best friend and companion. I was working sixty hours a week in the executive recruiting business, and felt that the idea of creating an organization that would inspire others to serve was a perfect outlet for all of the hurt and frustration I was dealing with in my personal life. It was not only a way to help others; it was also a way to help *myself*. I took all of my energy and pain and channeled it into the creation of Champions of Caring. For me, this became a healing process. Instead of focusing on the negative that I was experiencing, I was able to make something positive happen. Creating Champions of Caring helped me get through this difficult period, and fill my life with a new joy.

Networking: It's All About Whom You Know and Who Knows You

Energized by the meeting with Spielberg and my new idea for Champions of Caring, I made three calls. I realized that I had nothing to lose and everything to gain, so I went to the highest levels in Philadelphia.

First, I called Ed Rendell, then mayor of Philadelphia, and later governor of Pennsylvania. I knew that he was an advocate for children and community service, and that the concept would resonate with him.

Next, I called Cardinal Bevilacqua, the Archbishop of the Archdiocese of Philadelphia. I knew that Champions of Caring needed to cross religious and cultural boundaries. The lessons of the Holocaust are not Jewish lessons; they are human lessons.

Finally, I called David Hornbeck, the superintendent of the School District of Philadelphia.

I asked each of them to lend their names and support to Champions of Caring. I asked the cardinal and Hornbeck to allow me to circulate applications to their respective high schools to identify students who could be honored as Champions of Caring. They all agreed.

Lesson 1: The higher you go, the more likely you are to get support.

With these three calls under my belt, I pulled out my Rolodex, and began to call everyone I knew who I felt might be interested. In retrospect, I am sure that some of my friends thought that I had lost my mind. I went on endlessly about meeting Spielberg, and wanting to create this organization called Champions of Caring. I was wired and running on adrenaline. I soon realized that I needed to come back down to earth, and not bombard people with all of my ideas the minute I saw them. I had to take a deep breath and clearly determine what I needed, and who could help me.

I called an accountant friend for advice. A lawyer acquaintance helped me to attain not-for-profit status. At a party, I cornered an artist friend of mine whom I got to design our logo. I didn't want to become the woman that people avoided in the grocery store or on the street, thinking, "What does she want from me now?" But, I was also delighted that many people agreed to serve on my newly formed board and helped me make connections because they, too, believed in what I was doing.

> *Lesson 2: Not everyone will support you. Forget about the naysayers and surround yourself with people who believe in your mission.*

I carefully scripted myself for every call for support and request that I made. I had my passion and my vision, but I had to be able to communicate them to others and to explain how they could get involved. I began networking with educators, local and federal politicians, members of faith-based communities, the Bar Association, universities, sports teams, and foundations. I gave speeches locally, nationally and internationally—to *anyone* who would listen—and even to some who did so only reluctantly. Every time I was rejected or criticized, I remembered the lessons my father taught me, and kept going. You may not always get a "yes," but you may get someone to lend his or her name and support, and an introduction to that person's network of friends and colleagues. All you can do is ask.

The most difficult part of creating Champions of Caring was funding the organization. Support does not always equate to funding, and gaining funding has not been easy. But there have been several moments throughout this process that have truly been extraordinary. I recognize that without these gifts and these lucky moments, Champions still would have happened, but it would have taken longer, with a few more rejections along the way.

A good friend of mine was turning fifty-five, and wanted to mark the occasion in a very special way. She invited ten of her closest friends to lunch, where we each found an envelope on our plates. Opening them as instructed, we were stunned to each find a check for $5,500. Our friend explained that she wanted us to donate this money to our favorite cause—or better yet, start one of our own. I was thrilled when two women who had learned about Champions of Caring gave me their checks as well. It has NEVER been that easy to raise money again.

So, with initial seed-money, the idea for Champions of Caring seemed more doable than ever, and I began seeing a world of possibilities. I started working with high schools to motivate students to write essays describing their efforts to make the world a better place. I envisioned that the media would see this as simply *amazing* and put these kids up on pedestals. I truly believed that they would focus on these extraordinary kids—these new role models society so desperately needed.

Lesson 3: The media will not conform to your vision. Have a back-up plan.

Although I had started to garner support, the media and the broader community did not share my enthusiasm to get involved. So, I thought, if you can't get what you want, change what you need. The fundamental model of Champions of Caring still seemed sound; it just needed a little tweaking. Two years after our initial meeting, I mustered the courage to go back to Spielberg. I assumed that with his clout, the concept would gain the attention I knew it deserved. So I wrote him again, this time about my accomplishments. I told him that I had created a nonprofit foundation in Philadelphia that celebrated the great contributions of the city's selfless youth.

I told him that these kids were enthusiastically volunteering their time to help others in schools, hospitals, hospices, shelters, senior centers, and neighborhoods. They were initiating their own unique projects that were changing lives and dramatically impacting their communities. Most importantly, I wrote with great humility that this fledgling organization desperately needed support. My implicit message: I've done what you asked. Now could you please fulfill your promise to help me?

But Spielberg had other ideas. His response was along the lines of: "Okay, now I want you to creatively market these young people so that they are recognized as true heroes of their time. Let me know what you come up with."

Lesson 4: Nothing is easy.

Frustrated, but undeterred, I knew what I had to do. From past experience, I knew that I had to go to the one place that never fails me when I need a network of experts. Where people can get quick legal advice, financial tips, physician referrals, contractor recommendations and overall support and affirmation for whatever they happen to need at the moment: the beauty parlor.

"Pedicure!" I said to myself. And that's how Champions of Caring got its second big break. A friend, who is a Philadelphia television news anchorwoman, walked in and sat in the chair next to mine. During the exchange of pleasantries that only people who have had their feet exfoliated simultaneously can understand, I said, "Listen, I'm desperate to please Steven Spielberg."

She looked at me unblinkingly and said, "Go on."

I told her that in the next forty-five minutes she had to help me come up with a creative way to make heroes of our kids. Undaunted, she rubbed her hands together gleefully and said, "We are *so* going to rise to this occasion."

And there, amid the scent of nail polish and acetone, we hatched the idea to ask Philadelphia transit officials to let us broadcast the accomplishments of our kids on posters mounted on the backs of buses, inside trains, and on the walls of subway stations. The posters would read "Be a hero of your generation. Become a Champion of Caring."

Long story short, the transit people loved the idea. Spielberg liked it, funded it through his Righteous Persons Foundation, and before you could say *E.T.*, hundreds of buses all over Philadelphia boasted pictures of our kids. I became known as the "back of the bus lady," and schools throughout the city joined what was about to become a regional organization attracting students from all over the greater-Philadelphia area.

So, you might be thinking, "I will never be in a room with Steven Spielberg, and I definitely don't have a friend who is going to give me a $5,500 gift." I realize that these opportunities were extraordinary, and I'm thankful to have friends whom I have known for over thirty years (with the exception of Spielberg) for their generosity. But they explained that it was my *passion* and *tenacity* that attracted them. Even with these resources and chance encounters, it is about one's commitment and energy. These were the sparks, but I am certain that even without them my passion simply would have smoldered a bit longer before flaming. At some point, another spark would have struck fire. Lightning bolts are nice, but they're not essential.

And so, with the faces of our Champions displayed on buses throughout Philadelphia, and my new nickname, the "Back of the Bus Lady," Champions of Caring was in its beginning stages. Little did I know then the path that the next fifteen years would take, and how rewarding it would be for me.

Lesson 5: Sometimes the mission takes over.

Making the Most of It: Dealing with Life's Challenges

I became obsessed with the desire to change young peoples' lives by teaching them the skills to make the world a better place. It wasn't easy and there were a lot of setbacks, but I saw each one as a challenge to do better. I learned to celebrate the accomplishments of our Champions, the victories of gaining funding, and more importantly, I learned to *let go* of disappointments. Fulfilling the mission was key, and necessitated getting over hurdles to move forward.

Unfortunately, life sometimes gets in the way. One of my dearest friends, Adele, has frequently said to me when I share some of my hardships with her, "In life, you don't get what you deserve and you don't get what you want—you get what you get and you have to make the most of it." Well, after going through my divorce, I was not ready for what hit me next, but it's become an all too familiar story these days.

My ex-husband and I had been very friendly with a man whom we both loved and trusted. We traveled with him and his wife, shared holidays, spent New Year's Eve together and went out socially almost every weekend. He knew my parents, my brother, and my children, and we considered him family. He had convinced my husband and me, as well as my parents and brother, to put our money into a credit union of which he was the treasurer. It turned out that he had stolen this money. When I learned about this and later found out that many of his other close friends were also victims of this scheme, I became enraged. Collectively, he had stolen millions of dollars.

What concerned me the most was sharing this horrendous news with my parents. At the time, they were in their mid-seventies, and I was worried that the news would make them ill. I drove to New York and met my brother at their apartment. When I walked into the apartment, my parents saw my face and said, "What's wrong? Tell us immediately." I shared with them what had happened and how we had lost a substantial amount of our life savings. My father looked at me and said, "We are Holocaust survivors. Your mother was in Auschwitz. I was on a death march. *That* was a problem. This is just about losing money. We will get over it."

He then said something that I will never forget: "You don't say Kaddish (the Jewish prayer for the dead) over money." My brother and I were stunned to hear this reaction. Our father had been putting his money into this credit union over many years, and since he was retired, it was unlikely that he would ever recover his losses. And yet, he did not focus on this.

Relieved, I left the apartment to drive home to Philadelphia. When I got to the street, I started looking for my car. It was nowhere in sight. I thought I was losing my mind, and walked several blocks around their neighborhood to find it. There was no sign of my car, and finally, I realized it had been stolen. I burst into tears. Then, I went to the police station to report the theft, hoping to get some solace. Instead I heard, "Oh, this is the eighty-sixth car stolen this month. You people need to be more careful."

Utterly deflated, I rented a car and drove back to Philadelphia. Seeing how my father had handled the news about his stolen money, I stopped feeling sorry for myself. I realized how transitory money can be. I had worked so hard at establishing my business to earn this money, and in an instant, it was gone. At that point, I knew I needed to pursue a career that was more substantive and would make a greater impact on society. I needed fulfillment from my work that was more than financial, and would feed my soul.

Once again, I learned firsthand from my parents how to deal with crises, and keep my head high. My mother always told me that the most important skill you need to learn is *coping*. She used to say that it's easy to be happy when everything is going your way, but when the tough times come, you need to deal with the pain with a sense of dignity and grace. I threw myself even deeper into developing Champions of Caring.

Finding My Champions

Many a day I have thought, "What am I doing with my life?" I was never prepared for everything that went into creating and running a nonprofit organization. I had experience as an educator, entrepreneur, and public speaker, and had chaired various boards, but I still needed others to make Champions a success. I needed to seek out people who understood my mission and were willing to help. I could never actualize my vision by myself. Life was feeling difficult. The events of the past year, from my divorce to losing much of my savings and my family's savings to a friend who cheated us, made me feel very frightened and vulnerable. I prayed better things would start happening. I knew staying focused on my mission and being involved with my parents, children and friends would help me get through this difficult time.

Thankfully, my prayers for better things to start happening were answered when I met David Rosenberg, and his wife Margie. I was introduced to David by a mutual friend. When we first met, David told me that he had about forty-five minutes for lunch. I started telling him my story. David became intrigued and asked lots of questions. He then called his secretary and instructed her to cancel all of his appointments for the day. Four hours later, we were still sitting in that restaurant.

David and Margie would later accompany me and my parents as we took 200 Philadelphia high school students to the U.S. Holocaust Memorial Museum in Washington, DC. He heard my mother speak about her experiences in the concentration camps, and my father told him about Oskar Schindler.

David has told me over the years that this experience transformed him. Because of his interest, David joined the board of Champions of Caring, and became its chairman. He has since empowered us to grow and impact over 10,000 students here in Philadelphia, as well as the recipients of their service projects, and the teachers and administrators who support them. His friendship and leadership of the board are a blessing. His guidance and advice have steered me to make good decisions and avoid potential mistakes.

Passion Begets Passion

I never dreamt that following my passion would lead to passion and love. I met my future husband, Larry Shaiman, yes, through a personal ad. At the time, this was very shocking because (a) I would never have believed that I would write a personal ad, and (b) after twenty-five years of marriage, I was clueless about the dating world.

During our first conversation, Larry had three questions he used to screen me to see if we were compatible:

1) Was I an Eagles fan? (I asked if they played baseball or basketball, and later learned they are Philadelphia's football team.)
2) Did I love boating? (I told him I get seasick.)

3) Was I a Republican? (No, a registered Democrat.)

His response was "Let's get together anyway. You never know. We could wind up liking each other and even get married. Weirder things have happened."

I thought it was a bizarre conversation, but agreed to meet him. What did I have to lose? The rest is history. We were married within three years. Larry became the lawyer for Champions of Caring, *pro bono,* of course. He was my advisor regarding legal matters, and also a great supporter of the organization. By marrying Larry, I also got three wonderful daughters, Cindy, Pam, and Shira, and their spouses and families. But best of all is the addition of four more incredible grandchildren.

You never know what can happen when you follow your passion.

Getting Money: The Right Place at the Right Time

Three years into the Champions of Caring program, I was down to $500 in the bank. I was devastated. I had worked tirelessly and lovingly to create this organization. I didn't know what to do. I felt that I couldn't trouble the people who had just given me money, and yet I hadn't been successful in procuring enough grant money.

During that time, I was invited to give a speech for the Sabbath service at a synagogue outside of Philadelphia. I had been in California on business all week (I was still running my recruiting firm), and was really exhausted. I did not want to spend Friday night giving a speech. I wanted to go home and relax. But the people from the synagogue desperately needed me to come because they had no one else to replace a speaker who had backed out.

Reluctantly, I said yes. As it turned out, there was a horrible rainstorm, and I got lost on my way to the synagogue. I arrived late, drenched, and increasingly unhappy that I hadn't just gone home. To my amazement there were only ten people at the service. I was frustrated and angry. I thought, let me just give my speech and go home.

I dried off as best I could, put a smile on my face, and got up and delivered my speech with passion. These people had come out to hear me and they deserved my best. After the service, I was trying to quietly leave, when a man approached me and said "Come, let's sit here and have a cup of tea." I politely said no, but he persisted, and after a few minutes of my resisting, he finally blurted out, "I love what you are doing. Do you need money?"

Did I need money? What a question! We sat down, and he explained that he was on the board of a local family foundation. He invited me to come and present to his board the following Monday. After hearing my mission, the board gave me $30,000 and said that they would match dollar-for-dollar whatever I raised that year. I was stunned and filled with gratitude.

Lesson 6: Speak anywhere, anytime, and to anyone. You just never know.

The Nuts and Bolts of Champions of Caring

The first program that I created for Champions of Caring was the Recognition Program. Using Spielberg's language, "The Heroes of Our Time," we created an application book, which was distributed to hundreds of schools and organizations. Any high school student in our region who had participated in sustained community service could apply to be recognized as a "Champion."

Students had to document their service, and write a 500 word essay reflecting on what they had done, the impact it had, and how it changed them as a person. They also had to submit two letters of reference from people who were familiar with their service.

I put together a committee comprised of twenty educators from the School District of Philadelphia and the Archdiocese of Philadelphia, and we created a tool to evaluate the applications and review the reflection essays.

I'll never forget the first year we judged the students' essays. The meeting was scheduled for 5:00 PM on a Tuesday. That day, I was in New York interviewing candidates for my executive search firm. When I came out of my meeting, I couldn't believe my eyes. Because *once again* my car had been stolen. This time, in midtown Manhattan, in broad daylight. I felt violated and angry. I rented a car and drove in pouring rain, *again*, to Philadelphia. I was not in the mood to read any essays. My committee told me to go home and relax, and that they would review the applications. I said that because I was there, I might as well stay.

Right from the beginning, the essays were more than I had ever expected. Reading the words of these young people gave me a sense of hope that they would, in fact, create a better world. I quickly forgot about my stolen car and felt such comfort from the words of these Champions.

Jason, a student from an archdiocesan school, wrote about his experiences volunteering in Mexico, and how that had changed his life:

> *Through my volunteer work, I learned a lot about myself and life in general. What struck me most was the willingness of the citizens to give up a full day of work to benefit the community… Having grown up in a materialistic society and living a "comfortable life," it amazed me how the people drew their strength and hope from the community, and that is where their comfort was found. The importance of the community and the individual's contributions are aspects of their lives that they accept as part of survival. Not only survival of the body, but survival of the soul.*

Another teen, Tyaira, explained how it was her own neighborhood that had inspired her to get involved in service, and how these experiences had changed her:

> *I grew up in a rough neighborhood, and I have really seen a lot. I am one of those people who would like to see things change in my neighborhood. I would like to see the*

> *headlines in the newspaper say, "A six-year-old boy makes*
> *a change in his community," instead of "A six-year-old boy*
> *gets gunned down on his way to school." I believe that my*
> *service has made me a better and stronger person. It has*
> *made me see more in life. I believe there is so much more*
> *to life than just trying to make a living and staying alive.*
> *Life itself is a blessing, and in return for this blessing,*
> *I will work to make the world a better place. Working*
> *with the sick, I realize how fortunate I am. I choose not*
> *to complain.*

These became our first honorees. We later organized an annual event in the spring to honor and celebrate these students. We invited the mayor, cardinal, superintendents, teachers, family, friends, and supporters to attend. We also called the media to interview and promote these students. From 1995 to 2009, we honored over 2,500 students who have given over 750,000 hours of service. Drexel University has provided us with the venue for this event, and presented over $250,000 in scholarships to our Champions in recognition of their commitment to service.

For anyone who has attended one of these ceremonies, it truly is a touching event. To see the students run the entire program, and share how they changed the world is inspirational. And to witness the pride felt by their parents and teachers is deeply gratifying. Some of these students have never been acknowledged for anything. This is often the proudest moment of their young lives.

The Many Faces of Our Champions

What is immediately apparent is the diversity of these Champions. They are black, white, Hispanic, Jewish, Christian, and Muslim. They are confident, and they are shy. Some come to me with a master plan for how they are going to change the world. Others simply know that they want to "do something" because of their involvement in service projects. Champions of Caring gives them the motivation and tools to find that something.

Over the years, many of Champions have come from at-risk families. Some have been in foster care. Some have lived in homeless shelters. Some have shared with me that their families do not have enough money to buy food past the twentieth day of each month. Some have been abused, and some are "couch surfers," a term that I learned meant that they move from sleeping on the couch of one relative or friend to the next. Yet despite the hardships they are suffering in their own lives, they still serve others.

It is important to note that some of our Champions also come from the most affluent families in the greater-Philadelphia area. They seem to have all of the resources in the world. Yet many have told me about their problems with drugs, eating disorders, and the stress that they feel from the intense pressure to go to Ivy League colleges. Through their service projects, they have learned to look outside their "bubble worlds" and see the reality of others.

They are *all* Champions. In spite of their differences, they are connected by one thing: their hearts. They each have a commitment to improving themselves, their communities, and their worlds. They refuse to stand by silent and indifferent.

After creating the Recognition Program, we then partnered with the U.S. Holocaust Memorial Museum in Washington, D.C., to take students to witness what happens when the path of hate leads to genocide. Through Bob Wright at NBC, journalists like Andrea Mitchell, Ann Curry, and Lisa Myers, and political leaders like Senator Harris Wofford, came to the museum to address our students. They congratulated them for being the heroes of our time, and the students were amazed that these influential people would take the time to honor them for their service.

My mother was often the keynote speaker on our museum trips, and told her story to inspire these Champions to make the world a better place. The subjects of the dangers of hatred and indifference were always the cornerstones of her eloquent speeches:

> *I experienced great pain because people closed their eyes and hearts to my anguish and suffering. It is important to remember that some of the highest intelligentsia of German society masterminded the plan of our terrible destruction. They were PhD's and MD's who had taken an oath to heal and protect, and yet they used their knowledge to harm and destroy. During all of this horror, most of the world stood by silent and indifferent. It has been over sixty years since World War II has ended, and I had hoped that finally there would be some normalcy in our lives. But history travels very fast. And now, once again, we are facing war and violence.*

> *Hate is a disease that can be easily transmitted. I appeal to you, the young generation, to be on your guard. You hold the key to the future. You must fight for justice and be vigilant citizens… Don't let those who hate dominate!*

I have seen students' lives transformed by this trip and her words. They are able to make connections between what happened during the Holocaust, and the injustices they see in their communities and the world. They are inspired to return to their communities and stand-up and speak-out. Through this trip, both their hearts *and* minds are educated.

Ambassadors of Caring: Developing Social Entrepreneurs

A few years into doing this work, I was very content with the Champions of Caring Recognition Program. I had found my passion, created an organization that I was deeply proud of, honored my parents' legacy, and received support from Steven Spielberg. I had promoted young people throughout the greater-Philadelphia area as heroes, and also recruited a few hundred people to help. I thought that my concept was good and that my mission was strong. Leave it to a group of teenagers to tell me otherwise…

In my third year of Champions of Caring, a group of students complained that I wasn't doing enough. At first I was slightly offended.

"Not doing enough?" But I listened. The students said that they wanted to become social entrepreneurs. They wanted to learn the skills to take their service to a higher level and make an even greater impact. Some wanted to learn how to start their own nonprofit organizations. They wanted to become leaders, and learn grant-writing, advocacy, fundraising, budgeting, and public relations skills. They wanted to begin to address global issues. Out of this conversation, the Ambassadors of Caring Leadership Program was created.

The Ambassadors of Caring Leadership Program is a social entrepreneurship institute for students who have already been honored as Champions. The Ambassadors participate in a series of monthly retreats and workshops where they work with mentors and experts to create their own sustainable service projects. The beauty of this approach is that the projects evolve from what the students are passionate about, and then we teach them the skills to make their dreams a reality.

One student, Celine, who had recently lost her grandfather, wanted to honor his memory. Her approach was marvelously simple: She posted a note on a bulletin board at her school that read, "My grandfather just died, and I want to do something really special in his memory. If you'd like to help me brainstorm some ideas, please join me in room 311 after school." Ten kids showed up that afternoon. Today, more than 300 students at that high school are involved in community improvement, all because one girl was passionate about something. As Celine says, "Through doing this work, I have realized that the hope you give to others, you also give to yourself... I realize that with each hand I hold, story I hear, memory I share and smile I offer, I gain a hopeful energy—the energy of the human spirit in action."

And consider the example of Stephanie, who at age fifteen noticed that a disturbingly large number of elementary school students in her inner-city neighborhood were being promoted from one grade to the next without actually being able to read at the appropriate grade-level. So she took it upon herself to create a literacy program. Stephanie independently persuaded a neighborhood church to provide classroom space, recruited volunteer tutors, and put out the word that free help was available every afternoon for those who needed to improve their reading skills. Within three years, 400 students caught up to reading at grade-level because one girl saw something she didn't like and felt sure that she could do something about it. In early 2002, President George W. Bush called on Americans to devote 4,000 hours of service to their communities. He came to Philadelphia that spring to encourage volunteer work and national service as "part of a complete life." Stephanie, who was chosen to participate in the panel with him that day, proudly informed the president that Philadelphia's Champions of Caring had volunteered many *hundreds of thousands* of hours to their community already. The president smiled and appeared to be touched by her confidence and courage.

Over the years, the Ambassadors of Caring Program has gone on to partner with Drexel University, the University of Pennsylvania, Temple University, Bryn Mawr College, Villanova University, the Young Lawyers Division of the Philadelphia Bar Association, State Farm Insurance, and even local sports teams. Public relations and marketing experts, human resource specialists, accountants, and grant-writers were brought in to teach our Ambassadors the skills they needed to create their projects. Ambassadors have addressed a wide range of local and global issues, including literacy, hunger, health care, poverty, homelessness, violence, and the environment. They have presented their stories at local and national conferences, been interviewed by the media, and created their own not-for-profit organizations.

After developing the Ambassadors of Caring program, I realized that my passion was creeping into my work life. I gave up my search firm. I wanted to focus all of my energies on creating programs for Champions of Caring. The Ambassadors program gave me a way to teach all of the skills that I had learned through my professional career and the creation of Champions. It was an opportunity to teach the universal lessons of the Holocaust. I was running two powerful programs that were making an impact on many lives. I was truly living my legacy and teaching young people to live *theirs*.

Bringing Champions of Caring into the Classroom

One night, I woke up at 3:00 AM and had an *"A-Ha!"* moment. I realized that I was missing the mark. Champions of Caring was working with students who were already committed to service. They already "got it," and were doing the work. But, what about all of the other students in Philadelphia? I was not doing anything to educate and inspire them to get involved.

The next morning, I made another phone call to then Philadelphia school superintendent David Hornbeck. We set up a meeting, and I told him that I wanted to start teaching students in the Philadelphia schools to get involved in service. We strategized about how we could develop a curriculum that had academic rigor, met educational standards, and inspired young people to take action and create service-learning projects. I knew that this program needed to combine character education with service-learning methodology in order to teach both the values and dispositions necessary to make informed, responsible decisions.

I pulled together a team of experts from the School District of Philadelphia and the Archdiocesan Office of Education, and we began to create the Journey of a Champion School Program. We started by writing a grant, which was funded by the United States Department of Education, and then wrote a high school curriculum that taught both character education and service-learning skills. The Journey program teaches students to believe that they can make a difference. They are taught to consider the feelings and opinions of others, to have a sense of responsibility to help people, to care about issues in their communities, and to work to promote social justice. The Journey program also helps students identify their passion and create service-learning projects that address community needs by using their academic skills.

This program has been taught to over 6,000 students in eleven high schools throughout the greater-Philadelphia area. We also recently created the Middle Grades Curriculum, which has been taught in five Philadelphia middle schools. After learning from local police that most crimes committed by teenagers happen in the after-school hours, between 3:00 and 7:00 PM, we created the Champions of Caring

Club. This club provides an opportunity for students to be engaged in improving their communities during this potentially dangerous time.

Everyone Can Become a Champion

Our program has been taught in some of the toughest schools in Philadelphia, but what we've found over the years is that given a chance, some kids are driven to compassion in spite of themselves. Having driven my brand-new car to an inner-city school to introduce this new curriculum, one very tall, scowling teen approached me after I spent the class telling him about my family history and Champions of Caring. "I was gonna steal your car today, lady. But when I heard the story about your parents, I changed my mind. I thought I had it pretty tough, but I never met anyone whose whole family was killed." Then he awkwardly, but sincerely half-hugged me, and ambled away.

Sometimes a person can change the world by *not* doing something. Later, for his service project, my new friend became an exemplary mentor to a fatherless child. He became a Champion, and it started with one decision to not do something that would hurt another person. In this case, *me.* He turned his life around and wound up going to college, something he had never even considered.

Through the Journey of a Champion Program, I have had an opportunity to speak with students from many schools and many walks of life. I start by simply asking "Can you change the world?"

Silent at first, one student will usually say, "We're only in ninth grade. We can't change the world."

"Are you *sure?*" I ask.

Then something clicks. The examples usually start small: "Well, there's a kid in our class that everyone picks on and bullies. I always thought it was wrong, but I was scared to do anything about it. Maybe I'll speak up and not let people bully him anymore," one young man once told me.

"You're changing the world," I say.

And then the ripples grow, beyond their desks to the classrooms around them, to the schoolyard, and to the community at large.

Going Global

In 2007, I was in South Africa with my husband for a special milestone birthday. Within hours of arriving in Cape Town, jet-lagged and exhausted, I overheard a tour guide at the hotel mentioning a Holocaust Museum. I jumped in: "Excuse me, did you say Holocaust Museum?" "Yes," he said. "There is a wonderful Holocaust Museum. But it closes in about an hour."

I ran around the hotel, found my husband, and rushed to the museum. When we made it inside, I noticed a group of black South African teenage girls being escorted through the museum by a docent. I began to follow the group. As they passed the exhibit on Auschwitz, and then Oskar Schindler, I had to speak up. "My mother was incarcerated in Auschwitz," I said, "and my father worked for Schindler." Before I knew it, I was on stage speaking in front of this group. I spoke about my family's history. We talked about apartheid, and their lives, and then I told them about Champions of Caring and what I was doing in the United States.

The director of the museum, probably curious about who this woman was on his stage, approached me after my speech. He told me about Ma Afrika Tikkun, a national non-governmental organization, whose mission is to transform South African communities by working with young people and orphans. The honorary chairmen of the organization are Nelson Mandela and the chief rabbi of South Africa.

By seven the next morning, I had received a call from the director of Ma Afrika Tikkun's educational programs. That evening, I spent four hours with her over dinner discussing the synergy between our programs. I then had the pleasure of meeting the founders of the organization, the Lubner family, and realized that this was an opportunity to take Champions to a global level.

A month after returning to the United States, we launched the Champions of Caring Ma Afrika Tikkun Global Program. Twenty South African teenagers and their facilitators participated in this pilot program, and communicated via e-mail with our Ambassadors in the United States. They talked about their daily lives and their commitment to improving their communities. The South African group organized an extraordinary community-cleanup program. They engaged political leaders and their local police.

The idea of creating a global program might sound daunting, but all it took to start it was passion for what I was doing, and a desire to share it with others. By taking my passion with me even to South Africa, I came home with extraordinary results.

Champions of Caring has come a long way since that day in the beauty parlor. It is quite amazing to me that out of the horror of my family's experiences during the Holocaust, I was able to create something positive and meaningful that would touch so many peoples' lives. Over the years, I have had the privilege of meeting and working with some of the most amazing young people—*more than 10,000 of them*. Their energy, dedication, and vision for a better world has humbled and astounded me. The teachers who work with these students are my heroes. They have helped to make our curriculum come alive. Arthur Newman, one of our teachers from Kensington International Business High School in Philadelphia, says, "This program changes lives. It positively touches everyone involved. Because of this program my students are better people and care more about their communities."

Getting It

What is it that enables these young people to take such important initiatives from concept to reality? They mobilize because they really *get it*. They have freed themselves to view their surroundings with a critical eye and realize that they are part of something much larger than themselves, and something they can care for, be proud of, and improve for future generations.

These are terrific young people to be sure, but they weren't born with superpowers or a wealth of resources at their disposal. But they have a greater awareness and, of equal importance, they are fearless. If, on their way to realizing their ideas and dreams someone tells them "No," what have they lost? Through that rejection, they gain an opportunity to approach their goals from another direction. The stories of my Champions beg an obvious question: If they get it, shouldn't we all?

CHAPTER 3 GUIDING QUESTIONS

- Have you identified a cause that you are passionate about?
- Have you ever approached someone that you felt was "out of your reach," such as a famous person, or politician? Did you get what you needed?
- What life-changing events have happened to you?
- What tough times have you experienced? How did you deal with them? Who supported you through these times?
- Did you ask people to help? If so, how did it work out? Do you feel comfortable asking for help?
- Where has your passion led you in the past?
- Are you a risk-taker?
- Can you ask for money to support a cause you believe in?
- Do you ask others for advice?
- Do you know people who inspire you? What do they do that inspires you?
- Have you ever written a grant or tried to get funding for something?
- Do you believe that you can change the world? How?
- Have you ever worked on a global project?

Barbara's mother, Carola Iserowski Greenspan, grandmother Golda Greenspan, and father, Henry Greenspan, Krakow, Poland, 1946.

The coral ring—Carola Greenspan's engagement ring.

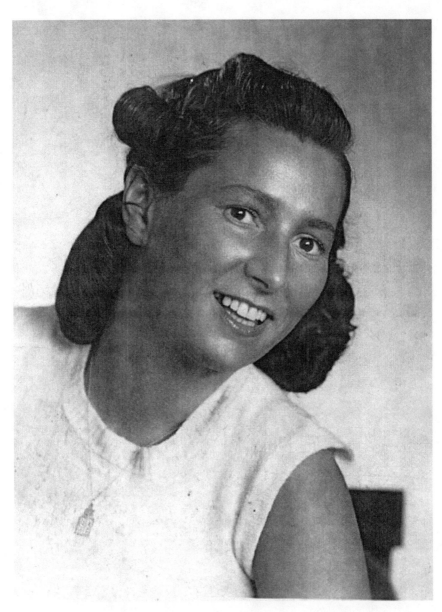

Carola Greenspan, Krakow, Poland, 1946.

Henry and Carola Greenspan's wedding,
Krakow, Poland, Lag BaOmer, May 1946.

Henry and Carola Greenspan,
Krakow, Poland, 1946.

Barbara Bella Greenspan, Regensburg, Germany, 1948.

Carola and Barbara
Greenspan, Regensburg,
Germany, 1950.

Barbara, Carola, Henry and Golda Greenspan,
New York City, 1957.

Golda, Joshua, Barbara, Henry and Carola Greenspan,
New York City, 1959.

Barbara and Joshua Greenspan, Catskill Mountains, New York, 1961.

Carola Greenspan, 1963.

Carola and Henry Greenspan, Joshua Greenspan,
and cousins Mark and Norman Doidge, 1966.

Barbara and Joshua Greenspan, Joshua's Bar Mitzvah, 1969.

Golda Greenspan, 1975.

Daughter Deborah Ryan, Carola Greenspan and Barbara, 1995.

Barbara and son Daniel Eisenbud, 1999.

Henry, Barbara, and Carola Greenspan, 2001.

Son-in-law Jeremy Ryan, grandson Jacob Ryan, daughter Deborah
Ryan, husband Larry Shaiman, brother Joshua Greenspan, Barbara,
Henry and Carola Greenspan, and son Daniel Eisenbud. Barbara and
Larry's wedding, April 6th, 2003.

Stepdaughters Shira Shaiman and Pam Dumont, daughter Deborah
Ryan, Barbara, Carola Greenspan, and stepdaughter Cindy Bamforth.
Barbara and Larry's wedding, April 6th, 2003.

Barbara and grandson Jacob Ryan, 2008.

Barbara and granddaughter Rebecca Ryan, 2008.

Grandchildren Madeline Dumont and Toby Pruskin, 2009.

PART II

Part II, Introduction

> *Am I going to let what is going on in the world out there determine who I am and what I do? Or am I going to let what's going on inside of me, in terms of my enthusiasm, my interests, my skills, my values, and my beliefs determine who I am and what I do?*
>
> —Richard Nelson Bolles, *What Color Is Your Parachute?*

I hope that sharing my story of how I am living my legacy through Champions of Caring has inspired and motivated you to reflect upon your own legacy—to look at your family history, your core values, and what you are doing every day to improve your life and the lives of others.

So often my friends and contemporaries reach a high point of frustration and discomfort at the notion that they ought to be doing more. They say things like, "How do you do it?" "Where do you find the time?" "I wish I felt that strongly or was that passionate about *something*!" "Where do you even *begin*?"

My answer is always the same: "Believe me. You are passionate about *something*. So what is it? Identify it and then use it! Start small." I don't expect everyone to start a not-for-profit organization. Living a legacy begins with simple steps to create meaning in your life and share it with others. If you have sadness in your life, do something to mitigate it. If you've been blessed, do something to celebrate it. There is no formula for building a legacy. No recipe exists, but there are essential ingredients: desire, vision, tenacity, commitment, and a *plan*.

You may be thinking, "I volunteer for many different causes, isn't that what living my legacy is all about?" If you are already volunteering your time, *bravo*. But living your legacy is more than that. Take a moment to reflect on the work that you are currently doing. Does this work really represent your core values? Is it addressing the issue that you are most passionate about, or is it a project that you fell into? What about this involvement do you like? Or, are you no longer finding the work fulfilling, and you serve out of habit or guilt? Are your skills being best utilized, or is there something else that you could be doing? Do you feel that your voice is heard and your ideas are respected and implemented? Are you making a meaningful contribution?

You might also be thinking, "I barely have enough time to spend with my family and friends, how can I do anything more?" My answer is simple: Involve them in your projects. Create projects together. Open up dialogue about the issues that you are passionate about. This enriches your experience, and shares your legacy with others.

Part II will help you to begin to live your legacy now! After reading the inspiring stories of people of all ages who are living their legacies, and learning some suggestions for getting started, you will be asked to complete a self-assessment called a Legacy Profile. You will then be able to create a plan for initiating your legacy. The second step of this process is finding ways to engage in service. My Ten Steps and Tips for Social Entrepreneurs will guide you through the process of creating a project, regardless of your time constraints. Finally, you will learn how you can share this legacy with others by composing Legacy Letters and establishing Legacy Clubs.

Regardless of your age or stage of life—whether you are a teenager, young professional, married with a family, a baby boomer close to retirement, or a retiree—you can begin to live your legacy now!

Chapter 4. LIVING YOUR LEGACY AT ANY AGE OR STAGE

We've all heard about everyday people who have righted wrongs, or single-handedly made a difference in someone's life. We read countless stories of people who zealously take up a cause after enduring an injustice or tragedy. But creating a legacy is not always just about what you *do*. It is not about individual actions. It is the core of who you are, how you act, and how you react in life—at home and in business, in private and in public. At every stage of your life, you can evaluate how much involvement makes sense for you. At some stages you might have more time, at others, less. But throughout your life, you should have something beyond your own needs that gives you a *purpose*.

I have compiled some of my favorite stories of people at different ages and stages of life, and from varied backgrounds, who are taking action every day to live their legacies. Each of these individuals has their own source of inspiration. As you read their stories, reflect on your own passion and skills, and the causes that you care about.

Champions of Caring: Teens Living Their Legacies

Raul

At age fifteen, Raul joined the Ambassadors of Caring Leadership Program. He was shy and quiet, and although he was active in service, he had never taken the lead on a project. For the first few months that I knew Raul, he could not come up with an idea for a service project. Every time I saw him I would nudge him and say, "Raul, what is your passion?" He would shrug and say, "All I really know how to do is salsa dance. But what can I do with *that*?" For a few months, Raul struggled with how to use his salsa-dancing skills to address an authentic need in his community. Then one day it hit him: "Ms. Barbara, I figured it out: I've noticed that in my community, there are bad relationships between teenagers and older people. Teenagers think that the seniors are boring, and the seniors think that teens are all criminals. I don't have grandparents, and some of my friends don't either, and I think it is important to have a relationship with older people. I think I can use salsa dancing as a way to bring my peers and the seniors in my community together!"

Raul immediately turned his excitement into action. He contacted the director of a local community center and asked if she would be interested in developing an intergenerational program where teens taught the seniors how to dance. He recruited twenty-one of his peers who also liked to dance, and teachers from his school to support the project.

Raul and his friends began by doing intergenerational interviews, discussing the seniors' experiences as teenagers, and their views on the youth of today. What the students soon learned was that many of the seniors loved to dance when they were young. In their next meeting, Raul and his friends began to teach the seniors the basic salsa steps. The seniors were so excited by this that in return, they wanted to teach the teens the jitterbug.

Raul was thrilled, but he didn't stop there. He wanted to share this experience with others and get the community involved. He took the information that they collected through the interviews, and created a book to share with his school and the greater community. Raul began to write letters to local businesses to get donations and financial support for their projects so that he could assist with renovating the senior center.

At the Champions of Caring Recognition Program the following year, Ms. Jane, one of the seniors that Raul worked with, joined us onstage and shared with the audience how this program had changed her:

> *This experience helped the seniors to see what life is like through young peoples' eyes and promoted understanding between the generations. We read so many negative stories about young people. It helped to change our attitudes about the youth of Philadelphia and to feel more comfortable around young people in our neighborhoods.*

In the second year of this project, Raul recruited students from two other high schools in Philadelphia and trained them so that they could make a difference in the lives of other groups of seniors.

Raul is a perfect example of how someone can use what they are passionate about—in his case, salsa dancing—to develop a service project that breaks down barriers and has a positive impact on all of those involved.

Christine

Christine was involved in service and volunteering in her community, but wanted to do something that had a larger global impact. During her junior year of high school, Christine set out to find a cause that she could address with her classmates. Through her research, she was shocked and angered to learn about child-soldiering in Uganda. She discovered that children as young as seven-years-old are sold as sex slaves or trained as soldiers and forced to kill. Christine realized that even though this did not affect her community, she had a responsibility as a *global citizen*. This was an important social justice issue that hadn't received enough attention, so she set out to raise awareness among her peers.

Christine was motivated to do something about this, but knew that it would be difficult to make changes and address a problem in a different country without a partner. Through her Internet research, she found and contacted the United Movement to End Child Soldiering, a peace-making and humanitarian organization, and explained that she wanted to get involved. With a group of her peers, she organized a gala to raise funds to benefit the organization. Over 200 people attended, and she raised more than $8,000. With this money, she was able sponsor the education of a former child soldier.

One of the messages that I always share with Champions is that there is a difference between *charity* and *change*. You can give charity, which is a short-term solution to a larger problem, or you can work to create change. By combining raising awareness with raising money, Christine did both. She is an example of how we can work locally to create global change.

Ryan

In honor of his Bar Mitzvah, Ryan collected and donated 1,200 books and 600 videos to inner city schools to combat illiteracy. He approached SEPTA, his local public transportation system, to help him deliver the books. After seeing the impact that this book collection made, he was inspired to do more. As an Ambassador of Caring, he teamed up with three other Champions and figured out how to collect and distribute 20,000 books. Once again, they engaged the transit system as a community partner to help with the distribution of the books.

In his next project, Ryan decided that he wanted to use the skills that he had learned to address a different issue: bullying. He also wanted to move from behind the scenes to a more public leadership role, as a peer mentor. When he learned that bullying and cyber-bullying were growing problems among middle and elementary school students in his community, he created a bullying workshop for fourth and fifth graders. He recruited and trained ten of his peers to help lead the workshops. The group educated the students about conflict resolution, cyber-bullying, and how to handle bullies.

In his senior year, Ryan used all of his new social entrepreneurship skills to take on an even greater challenge. He designed and managed a school-wide health fair. He partnered with a local hospital and planned an event to educate 600 of his peers about issues such as anorexia, bulimia, HIV/AIDS, and healthy eating and exercise.

As Ryan's passions and interest changed, he was able to use the skills that he had learned to address a variety of important issues. Whenever he recognized a new problem or need in his community, he took action. He also developed his public-speaking skills and became the emcee of our awards ceremony addressing an audience of 500 people.

Madeline

After learning about the genocide in Darfur and attending a speech presented by a refugee from Sudan, Madeline, an eighth-grader, was inspired to raise awareness about this important issue among her peers. She was tired of the lunchroom conversations focusing on the latest celebrity news and dating gossip, and wanted to find a way to encourage her friends to discuss more important matters.

Being a *fashionista*, she knew that one way to gain the attention of her friends was to create a clothing trend. So, with the help of a local designer and a t-shirt printing company, she created a "Hate Is Out of Style – Save Darfur" t-shirt campaign. Madeline set up a table in her school cafeteria, and quickly sold-out of her first batch of fifty shirts.

In the second year of her project, Madeline created two new designs and expanded her project to increase awareness within her school and community. She attached a fact sheet about Darfur to each t-shirt she sold to ensure that her customers were well informed. She also began to engage in advocacy work beyond selling the t-shirts. In two years, Madeline raised over $3,000 through this project and donated all of the funds to non-profit organizations that advocate for peace, and provide resources to refugees in Darfur.

Madeline is truly a social entrepreneur. By using her creativity, leadership abilities, and networking skills, she was able to take her interest in fashion and address a global concern. Her t-shirt business raised funds, but more importantly, *promoted awareness* about this important cause.

Ambassadors Collaborating

Some of the most powerful projects that I've seen are collaborations between students from different backgrounds and communities. Our students from the suburbs and inner- city are sometimes surprised to learn that there are similar problems in their communities, including teen pregnancy, sexually transmitted diseases, depression, unhealthy eating, and low self-esteem.

One year, in our Ambassadors of Caring Program, Jill and Sarah, from a suburban area, and Jasmine, from one of Philadelphia's toughest neighborhoods, collaborated to create a program to foster self-esteem in young girls in their respective communities. They worked together to brainstorm ideas for programs and activities that could be used. The suburban group contacted a local elementary school and organized monthly workshops for at-risk girls. The Philadelphia-based group created a program called "Save the Sisters" to teach their peers how to succeed in high school, go on to college, and avoid getting pregnant, and using drugs.

In creating these service projects, the girls were able not only to make positive changes in their own communities, but it was also an opportunity for them to expand their worldviews from their neighborhoods and learn about the universality of some of the issues facing our society. The collaboration broke down barriers, created new friendships, and promoted respect.

Terrell

Terrell, an alumnus of Champions of Caring, became involved in service at a young age, and recognized very early on that his strength was in leading and mentoring others. Through a variety of service projects throughout his teenage years, Terrell honed his public speaking and leadership skills. He knew that his strength was not just his ability to volunteer his own time, but to motivate and lead others to serve as well.

Terrell is now twenty-seven years old, and employed by a major corporation. Although his job keeps him very busy, he finds time to give back to the community where he grew up. Terrell found his passion from his own personal experience of being raised by a single mother in Philadelphia. He created an organization called Program Watch, which works with inner-city boys and teens being raised by single mothers to provide them with mentoring, life coaching, community service opportunities, and work readiness skills.

Terrell frequently speaks at Champions of Caring events, serving as a role model and inspiration to other young people to serve.

Champions at All Ages and Stages

One important lesson I quickly learned from those who strive to improve their communities is that it is an ageless pursuit. I have met inspirational adults *of all ages and walks of life* who have selflessly contributed to the greater good. Of course, all of these individuals are not part of Champions of Caring, but they are proof that there is no statute of limitations when it comes to giving back. Here are some examples of individuals who have inspired me:

Jeremy

Many people begin their journey as volunteers because of a cause that is personal to them. Jeremy, a lawyer and father of two young children, decided to join the board of the small agency that had taken care of his uncle who suffered from cerebral palsy and mental retardation.

Although Jeremy knew little about the details of research, treatment, and caretaking, he joined the board of the organization and brought his experience as a lawyer to become the head of the board's finance committee. His law firm, one of the largest in Philadelphia with offices in several cities, was very supportive of the time that he gave working with the board.

Alison

Often, living your legacy can be tied directly to your career. As a new English teacher and reading specialist in an inner-city school, Alison was already in a position where she was giving a great deal of herself to her students. She was dedicated to instilling a love of reading and writing in her students, but she knew that this was not enough. She did not have the resources or community support that she needed to make a true impact on her students. Her school had no library, and her local public library branch closed down. After petitioning her principal and the school district with no success, she decided to take matters into her own hands. She got together a group of ten of her friends, and asked them each to clean out their bookshelves, and ask their families and friends to do the same.

She then took it one step further. Because she usually hosted social events for friends, she added a twist to her next holiday party. On her invitation, she asked everyone to bring a book and a $5 donation to go towards purchasing bookshelves for her classroom. Within one month, Alison had collected several hundred books and several hundred dollars. This project became a tradition with her family and friends. By using her social network, Alison was able to find simple ways to involve her family and friends in her cause and support her efforts to empower her students.

Margie

A close friend of mine, Margie, once told me that one of her favorite hobbies was knitting, but she couldn't figure out what she could do with knitting to help others. She loved giving handmade blankets to her friends and family, and thought that maybe she could bring this same joy to others. After giving it some thought, she reached out to her friends, her seventy-five-year-old mother, a group of her mother's friends who also enjoyed knitting, and her own teenage children, and partnered with a women's shelter in Philadelphia. This was a place where formerly incarcerated women stayed before transitioning into living on their own within the community.

Together, the group knit blankets for the women at the shelter, to provide them with comfort and something to call their own when they reentered society. With each blanket, they attached a note of support for the recipient. The women who receive the blankets are moved by this personal gift, and appreciative that others care about them. The women who knit the blankets feel a sense of pride, and a special connection to one another and to the women that they are supporting. Everyone gains something special.

The Penniless Philanthropist

A group of single mothers whom I know participate in what they call "Penniless Philanthropy." Once or twice a year, they fill bags with their family's gently used clothes and accessories and participate in a clothing swap. They then take any items that are not selected in the swap and donate them to a local shelter. Each family gets new additions to their wardrobe and donates some of the money that they would have spent on clothes to the charity of their choice. The best part is, they are teaching this lesson to their children as well.

"For $20, I'm a Hero"

I have a friend who always buys tuna fish in large quantities when it's on sale. He has purchased as many as thirty cans at time. The employees of the grocery store always ask, "Is this for your cat? Do you have lots of cats?" What they don't know is that he takes the cans of tuna to local homeless shelters, and anonymously leaves them on the steps. When I asked him why he does this, his response was, "For twenty bucks, I'm a hero, and I've helped someone in need."

The Young Professional: Beyond Happy Hour

The best way to predict the future is to create it.
—Peter Drucker

Terrell, Alison, and Jeremy are just a few examples of people who are living their legacies as part of their professional and personal lives. They are dedicated to their jobs, but also find time to give back in ways that are connected to their careers, and may even benefit them professionally.

The young, single years are traditionally a time to define who you are and what you stand for. What better time to start to create your legacy? You might find that your job or personal relationships are not as fulfilling as you would like them to be. You may still be struggling to establish yourself professionally and to gain new skills and experiences. Maybe you were involved in service in high school, or college, and haven't found an organization to get involved with as an adult. Or, in your busy work and social schedule, you just haven't found a cause that you are passionate about yet. *Now* is the time to explore.

If you are just getting started:

- Get involved with a local volunteer group that interests you.
- Contact the community-relations department at work (if your organization has one), and find out about their projects or suggest a new project.
- Find people who can help you and increase your social network and establish new, fulfilling relationships in your life.
- Broaden your worldview. If there is a place that you have always wanted to visit but haven't been able to, look for service opportunities there. Incorporate

service into your travel plans. Look at a Web site like Voluntourism.org for ideas.

- Check out online organizations such as the International Young Professionals Foundation (iypf.org). It has members from over one hundred different countries, and inspires them to make positive changes in the world. Its focus is to meet the United Nation's Millennium Development goals, which include eight goals that the United Nation's has set out to meet by 2015, including eradicating extreme hunger, poverty, and combating HIV/AIDS and other diseases.

If you have already found your cause:

- Trade in happy hours and evenings out for activities that get your friends together to do good work.
- Create a club around a cause, or *several causes*, that are important to you.
- Get members of your religious community involved. Make it an interfaith collaboration if possible.
- Reconnect with your family and make the world a better place. Take the lead and create family traditions for your generation, like serving meals at a shelter on Thanksgiving.
- Make your project a way to learn a new skill and to challenge yourself. Get involved with a cause or a group and then write an article, help write a grant, or use desktop publishing to create a brochure or newsletter. Then add it to your resume.
- Encourage your co-workers to get involved. It may help you to stand out at work, and also hone your leadership skills.
- Celebrate your accomplishments and share them with family, friends and colleagues.

Most people who do service say that it adds a dimension to their lives that never existed. Getting involved in creating your legacy will add value and meaning to your life *and* create powerful relationships. You simply can't lose and you'll feel good about yourself.

Baby Boomers and Retirees: Reinventing and Revitalizing Your Lives

> *We are prone to judge success by the index of our salaries or the size of our automobiles, rather than by the quality of our service relationship to humanity.*
>
> —Reverend Dr. Martin Luther King Jr.

The task of keeping the soul young and living a legacy is of supreme relevance to baby boomers. Powerful in number, acquisitive by any measure, many have made their money, bought their homes, schooled their children, and now, for the first time, are feeling a bit mortal. They are wondering:

- Is this really *it?*
- Is this really all *there is?*
- Have I lived my life?
- Have I done it all?
- Am I leading a meaningful life?
- Am I a good parent, a good partner, a good friend, a good neighbor, a responsible citizen of my community and the world?

And suddenly they feel energized to do more. They may become intrigued at the thought of a whole new perspective on life and how to live it, for themselves and for others. For those who are suddenly thinking "legacy," but feeling as if they're down by three touchdowns late in the game, the news is good: It's not that hard. That's what this book is all about.

Marc Freedman, author of the book *Encore*, and founder of the Encore online community (encorecareers.org), is leading the movement for baby boomers to find work that matters in the second half of their lives. He encourages baby boomers to find "encore careers" that combine social contribution, personal meaning, and financial security.

Baby boomers are moving away from the idea of traditional retirement toward a new concept of reinventing themselves—particularly in these difficult financial times.

If you are not looking for a new career, consider other ways that you can get involved. Ask yourself how much time you are willing to commit to addressing the issues that are important to you. Are there several different causes that you want to explore before committing yourself to one? This is a good opportunity to reflect on your experiences, knowledge, skills, accomplishments, and what you enjoy doing in order to find new ways to live your legacy.

Here are five questions and suggestions to help you to clarify your thoughts:

1. What business skills did you learn throughout your career that you could apply to doing good?
2. If you are an empty-nester, what parenting skills or life experiences do you have that could help others? How can you teach your skills to others? Could you be a mentor to high school students? Or find a social services agency and volunteer for one of their adult literacy or parenting programs?
3. Was there a career path that you didn't take that you want to experience now? If you always dreamed of being an artist, now is the time to get involved in a local mural arts project, or volunteer to teach art in an after-school program. Find out if there are courses that you might need to take to prepare for this.
4. Get out of your comfort zone. Take that class; go on that trip. You never know whom you will meet or what impact they will have on your life. This might be a way to find new causes that you care about.
5. Join a network. The Corporation for National and Community Service (getinvolved.gov) has a variety of programs designed for retirees.

Chapter 5. CREATING YOUR LEGACY PROFILE

No matter what your age or life circumstances, living your legacy begins with asking yourself the following five fundamental questions:

1. Who am I?
2. What am I passionate about?
3. What are my skills?
4. What do I want to accomplish?
5. How can I live my legacy and share it with others?

Who Am I?

Identity is powerful and important. In order to know who you are and how you would like to be viewed by others, you must know where you have come from, what your values are, and who you want to become. I shared my personal journey—from growing up as the daughter of Holocaust survivors to becoming a teacher, an entrepreneur, and then a social entrepreneur and founding Champions of Caring—to help you reflect on your own journey.

Stop and explore your life to this point. What experiences drove you to shape the life you live today? Reflect, and then project. Consider your priorities, and your daily routine. Step outside your routine. Open your eyes. Is there something that bothers you that you aren't doing anything about? How many hours a day are you not being as productive as you could be? Are you filling your day with things that you are proud of, or are you spending it in pursuit of things that don't really matter? How many times have you said, "I don't know where the time went?"

In an age when so much time and energy are focused on money and material things, I can tell you from my own experiences that there is no greater joy or satisfaction than knowing that you have successfully addressed a cause or changed someone's life for the better.

Who Am I? Guiding Questions

- What are my core values?
- How did I acquire these values?
- What events have shaped my life?
- Who inspires me?
- What accomplishments am I most proud of?
- What roles do I play? (List them.)
- What are my priorities, and why are they important to me?
- What do I spend most of my time doing? (Write down a typical daily and weekly schedule.)
- What brings me the greatest satisfaction?
- Are there things that I spend time doing that I don't enjoy, or that are no longer important to me?
- What is my vision for a better world?

What Am I Passionate About?

Part of who we are is our passion. We each have a passion. For some of us this is *something we love to do:* salsa dancing, cooking, or playing sports. For others, it is something that we are passionate about addressing because *it angers us,* or has harmed us or one of our loved ones: violence, racism, illnesses, hunger, illiteracy, poverty. For some, it is *groups* we are passionate about: orphaned children, the elderly, our own families and friends.

The search for what resonates may not yield answers overnight. My parents' experiences and their impact on my upbringing set me on a path, but recounting the lessons of the Holocaust and living my parents' legacy were not a destination in itself. I knew that I was involved in important work all along, but it was not until Steven Spielberg inspired me to honor youth for their service that I would begin to truly embrace and live my legacy. I was fortunate that I had a catalyst to ignite my passion. Once my grandchildren were born, I became even more motivated to continue my work. I wanted them to grow up in a safer, kinder world. I wanted them to become Champions of Caring, and to live their legacies.

Whatever your passion is, there is a way to turn it into a way to serve others. Consider the examples of our Champion, Raul, who was passionate about salsa-dancing and cared about the elderly in his community—or Margie, who connected her love for knitting with her concern for women in shelters. By connecting their passions and concerns, they created dynamic projects.

What Am I Passionate About? Guiding Questions

- What do I love to do?
- What are my hobbies or interests?
- What would I love to spend more time doing?
- What groups am I interested in spending more time with, i.e., children, the elderly or members of my faith-based community?
- What problem or social issue upsets me and motivates me to take action?

What Are My Skills?

Ok, you might say, it is one thing to be passionate about a cause, but what can I really *do* about it? Take a personal skills inventory. Ask yourself what skills you already have that are transferable to what you want to do. Think of Jeremy, the lawyer who volunteered his legal skills to the organization that had helped his uncle.

What skills have you acquired through your career, hobbies, and leisure activities? I have also encouraged friends to think of all of the skills that have made them a great parent or grandparent and share them with others by being a mentor. In addition to sharing the skills you already possess, getting involved in your community can help you to learn new ones.

What Are My Skills? Guiding Questions

- What are the skills that I have acquired through my professional and personal life?
- Is there a need in the community that my skills can help support?
- What are the skills that I would like to further develop?
- Which skills do I have that I do not want to use or focus on? (For example, if you are an accountant, you may not want to be involved in crunching numbers, but would like to try something different and more creative.

Compose Your Life Backwards: What Do I Want to Accomplish?

We are trained to move forward in life. Society propels us. We think in terms of progress and advancement. As important as it seems to think about where your next step will take you, it is also important to think about what your choices *say* about you. Compose your life backwards. If you started at the finish line and worked retrospectively, would your decisions be the same? Would you spend your time the same way? What would you do differently?

While writing my own autobiography in Pittsfield so many years ago was a challenging task, it helped me to recognize who I really was and who I wanted to *be*. Think about what you might write in your autobiography ten, twenty, thirty, or forty years from now.

What Do I Want to Accomplish? Guiding Questions

- What do I stand for?
- How would I like for others to view me?
- What values would I like to pass on to my family and friends?
- What issue or cause would I like to address?
- What impact would I like to make on my community?

Putting It All Together

After you answer all of these questions, go back and summarize what you have learned about yourself. Take a few moments to reflect about how all of these pieces fit together. This will help you create your Legacy Profile: who you are, what you are passionate about, what skills you enjoy using, and what issues you want to address. Add one final group of questions: How can I live my legacy? Brainstorm ideas for how you can use this information to create a project that will bring you fulfillment and do something to improve your community. Here is an example of a Legacy Profile:

Who Am I?

- I am a retired corporate executive.
- I am a proud father, grandfather, and husband.
- I value time with my family, and leisure time on my own.
- I am a strong leader, and very patient.

What Am I Passionate About?

- I am passionate about playing golf. I would like to spend more time doing this in retirement.
- I am passionate about my family and sharing my values with them.
- I am interested in finding ways that I can give back to my community.

What Are My Skills?

- Managing people.
- Networking.
- Training/instructing others.

What Do I Want To Accomplish?

- I want to be a role model for my children and grandchildren.
- I would also like to do something to be a role model for young men.

How Can I Live My Legacy?

- I can sign up to become a mentor, and teach my mentee how to golf.
- I could bring my grandson along, and get to spend more time with him.
- I could also help to organize a golf tournament to raise money for my favorite cause.

This is just one example of how to create a personal profile. Maybe you are a busy mom, who also values spending more time with your women friends. This is a great opportunity to get together with your friends, discuss each of your unique skills, and identify a cause that you can address collectively—while spending time with one another and getting your children involved.

On the following pages, you will find worksheets to complete your own Legacy Profile. You may not have a response to every question, but use this as a guide to help you to design your personal plan. It is helpful to revisit this profile from time to time and add to it as you progress along the journey of living your legacy.

My Legacy Profile   **Date:**

Who Am I?

- What are my core values?

- How did I acquire these values?

- What events have shaped my life?

- Who inspires me?

- What accomplishments am I most proud of?

- What roles do I play? (List them.)

- What are my priorities, and why are they important to me?

- What do I spend most of my time doing? (Write down a typical daily and weekly schedule.)

- What brings me the greatest satisfaction?

- Are there things that I spend time doing that I don't enjoy, or that are no longer important to me?

- What is my vision for a better world?

What Am I Passionate About?

- What do I love to do?

- What are my hobbies or interests?

- What would I love to spend more time doing?

- What group am I interested in spending more time with?

- What problem or social issue upsets me and motivates me to take action?

What Are My Skills?

- What are the skills that I have acquired through my professional and personal life?

- Is there a need in the community that my skills can help support?

- What are the skills that I would like to further develop?

- Which skills do I have that I do not want to use or focus on?

Compose Your Life Backwards. What Do I Want to Accomplish?

- What do I stand for?

- How would I like for others to view me?

- What values would I like to pass on to my family and friends?

- What issue or cause would I like to address?

- What impact would I like to make on my community?

How Can I Live My Legacy?

Brainstorm some ways that you can combine your values, passion, skills, and life goals to begin to Live Your Legacy NOW!

- What is an issue that is important to me?

- How can I address this issue?

- What existing organization can I volunteer with that deals with this issue? Or, can I organize a new group?

- Whom can I involve in my efforts to address this issue?

- Looking back at my Legacy Profile, will this work help me to create the type of legacy that I want to live? Does it incorporate my passions, interests, and skills?

- How will I make an impact?

Living Your Legacy At Home, In the Community, and In the Workplace

Living your legacy can be integrated into your actions and practices at home, in the community and in your workplace. By doing this, you will begin to create cultures of caring—environments that are positive, inclusive, and allow you to give back to your community and contribute to the world around you. As you begin to think about living your legacy and designing service projects using the ten steps that you will learn in the next chapter, reflect upon how you will create cultures of caring in all areas of your life.

At Home

- How can you involve family members in your project?

- If there are children in your life, how can you involve them in this process? How can you design activities that build character and teach them the importance of giving back?

- What kinds of projects or traditions can you establish in your family? Can you make them intergenerational?

- How can you create a culture of caring in your home?

In the Community

- How can you get your friends involved? Can you turn social events with friends into opportunities to do good work?

- What groups or associations do you belong to? How can you involve other individuals in this work?

- Do you belong to a religious community? Can you involve other congregants in your project? Or, can you create opportunities for interfaith projects?

- How can you create a culture of caring in your community?

In the Workplace

- What is your vision for a better workplace?

- Is there a need in your workplace that you would like to address?

- What skills can you use to address this need?

- Whose support do you need to be successful?

- How will you determine if you are successful?

- How can you create a culture of caring in your workplace?

Chapter 6. TEN STEPS TO GETTING STARTED

Now that you have taken some time to reflect upon your core values, what you are passionate about, your skills, and what issue you want to address; it's time to take *action*. The next section outlines ten steps to help you get started. Whatever your time limitations and level of commitment, you can create a project that will make a difference. Do an honest assessment. Ask yourself how much time you have to commit. This will help you determine your level of involvement. You may fall into one of three categories: Beginner, Intermediate, or Advanced.

Beginner: You have limited time and are new to this type of work.

Intermediate: You have experience with service and feel ready to create a project of your own.

Advanced: You have a lot of experience with service projects and might consider starting your own not-for-profit organization.

Here are some examples of how you might address a cause, based on your level:

What is the Need?	Beginner	Intermediate	Advanced
Hunger	Volunteer once a month to cook dinner at a soup kitchen with your family.	Join the advisory board of the soup kitchen and organize a fundraising campaign.	Start a 501(c)(3) organization that increases awareness about hunger and raises money to provide healthful snacks for children in low income schools.
Teenage Pregnancy	Volunteer with a local mentoring organization and help build the self-esteem of a teenage girl.	Work with community partners to organize a one-day health fair at your local high school that teaches teens about sex education.	Create an organization that provides ongoing outreach and resources to teach self esteem, abstinence, and safer-sex practices in local communities and schools.
Literacy	Volunteer at an adult literacy organization.	Recruit your coworkers and create a tutoring program sponsored by your employer.	Start an organization that raises funds and advocates to improve literacy programs.

TEN STEPS TO GETTING STARTED

Step #1: Identify an Authentic Need

Step #2: Choose a Project

Step #3: Create Your Mission Statement

Step #4: Identify Community Partners

Step #5: Create an Action Plan and Timeline

Step #6: Develop a Budget and Fundraising Strategy

Step #7: Spread the Word

Step #8: Evaluate Your Progress

Step #9: Reflect

Step #10: Celebrate and Promote Your Successes

Step #1: Identify an Authentic Need

You may still be unsure of what you want to do. Or you might have an idea, but aren't sure if it's a worthwhile endeavor. Identifying authentic needs will help you get organized and focused.

Your need can be something small and local (think of the example of the tuna fish, or the penniless philanthropists), or something large and global (think of Christine and the child soldiering project). If you are already passionate and excited about a cause, that's a wonderful start. But be careful: It's easy to get carried away by your passion. First and foremost, it's important to make sure that there is actually a need for the project that you want to create, or that you are not replicating one that already exists.

I recently heard a joke about a teacher who asked his thirty students to go out and do a good deed in the community. When they returned to class, the teacher asked them to share what they had done. One by one, they stood and said, "I helped an old woman cross the street." After the thirtieth student repeated the same good deed, the teacher said, "I can't imagine that there were that many old women who needed to cross the street in our small community. Why did it take thirty of you to help her cross?" One young man responded: "Because she didn't want to cross the street."

Always make sure you are addressing an authentic need.

There are many ways to identify authentic needs. Here are a few:

- **Create a community "walk- or drive-about."** Take an afternoon, pick an area, walk around and simply observe. What do you see that needs improvement? What is missing? Are there enough parks and playgrounds in your community? Are there enough supermarkets? Is there accessible transportation? What resources are there in the community that could be shared with those less fortunate?

- **Go to the source**. If you are passionate about working with teens or seniors, talk to them about what resources or programs they would like to have, or what organizations they are already involved with. In my case, by talking with my Champions, I was able to recognize that there was a need for a program that taught leadership and social entrepreneurship skills. This led to the creation of the Ambassadors of Caring Leadership Program.

- **Look for stories in the newspaper, online, or on television about a specific issue that you are interested in**. This is particularly important for identifying a global need. For example, Christine, whom we discussed in the last chapter, learned about child-soldiering in Uganda and raised funds and awareness in her community about the issue.

- **Draw from your personal experience**. Are you, your family, or your friends directly affected by a need or an illness? Have you seen this firsthand? These stories can provide powerful testimonials. If someone in your family has suffered from a problem, you can create awareness about it.

For the Beginner:

- Find an existing organization or group that is addressing one of the needs that you identified.
- Research their accomplishments and find out if you are comfortable with the group and their values.

Complete columns 1—3 in the Identifying Authentic Needs Chart on page 109.
For the Intermediate or Advanced:

Do your research. You don't want to reinvent or replicate a program that already exists. Ask yourself the following:

- Are there programs in my community that currently address this need, or are doing something similar to what I am proposing?
- Are their missions and objectives similar to mine?
- Can I work comfortably with these groups or individuals?
- Can I improve or add to what they are already doing?
- Do I want to approach this issue from a different perspective, and therefore start my own group?

Complete all of the columns on the Identifying Authentic Needs Chart.

For the Advanced:

- Keep in mind that being able to identify an authentic need is also important when it comes to seeking funding to support your cause. You will need to defend your case, prove that your program is needed, and that you are adding value by creating this organization.

Identifying Authentic Needs Chart

Use the following chart to help you gather information about the need that you want to address, and determine what role you can play in addressing it.

Need	Evidence of Need	What is being done to address this need?	How can I get involved with these efforts?	How can I add value to what is currently being done to address this need?

Step 2: Choose a Project

There are many ways to address an issue. This is where your Legacy Profile comes into play. How you address your cause depends on your skills and interests. The way I choose to address an issue might be very different from what you are comfortable doing. Once you have identified an authentic need, you should determine which organizations you can work with that are involved with this cause, or what type of project you want to create. Also try to identify which aspects of the issue you wish to impact. You cannot solve world hunger, but you can address hunger issues in your community by working with a local soup kitchen or shelter. Or, you may not be able to serve in the kitchen during hours that it is open, but you can spearhead a fundraising campaign on a schedule that works for you.

BRAINSTORMING PROJECT IDEAS

Write down all the ideas that come to mind for possible projects. Don't filter them as you write them.

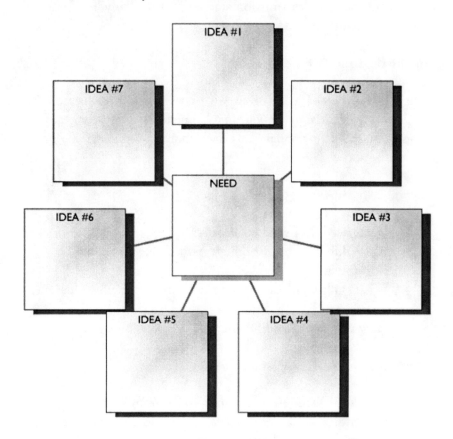

Step 3: Create Your Mission Statement

I live by the motto "Dream big and in Technicolor." It's wonderful to be a dreamer, but it is also important to set yourself up for success. To do this, you need a clear mission statement. Outline your vision, but be realistic about your goals.

For the Beginner:

Even if you are getting involved with an existing organization, you should still have a vision for your involvement. Your mission statement is more about your personal goals than about the mission of a project or organization.

Ask yourself:

- What need do I want to address?
- What kind of environment will I be comfortable working in?
- What skills will I use? What skills can I learn from this experience?
- How will I make a difference?

Sample mission statements for a Beginner project:

- I will address my environmental concerns by supporting the efforts of a local recycling agency to educate the community about the importance of recycling and "going green." I hope to learn how to create an effective public relations campaign, and become more comfortable with speaking publicly about this cause. I will dedicate five hours per month to this effort, and will focus on making sure that families in my neighborhood are recycling regularly.
- I will become involved with the PTA at my child's school. Because of my background in development and fundraising, I will work toward obtaining more resources for the school by working with community

partners. I will dedicate two evenings per month to meetings, as well as several hours per week working on projects.

For the Intermediate or Advanced:

Creating a mission statement requires time, thought, and planning. Going through this process will help you solidify the scope of your work and provide you with a clear outline of your goals.

- Mission statements should include:

   -A description of the project or group that you are starting.

   -The actions you plan to take.

   -What you want to accomplish.

- If this is a group project, have everyone write his or her own ideas down, and then work together to create the final statement.

- Once you have the basic ideas in writing, refine the language. Be clear and precise. You want to capture what you are doing in about three to four lines.

Sample mission statements for an Intermediate project:

- We are a group of concerned parents who will utilize our community connections to organize a traveling health fair to educate high school students about teen pregnancy and sexually transmitted disease prevention.

- Our committee of Corporation X employees will work to promote early childhood literacy by tutoring local elementary school students on a weekly basis and organizing an annual fundraiser to provide books to school libraries.

- High School X's baseball team players, parents, and coaches will partner with the local construction company to help inner-city high schools renovate their baseball fields. The project will promote dialogue between the students and parents from diverse communities.

For the Advanced:

Once you have created your statement, it should be printed on your advertising materials, newsletters, Web site, and grant requests and incorporated into any public speaking or presentations about your project.

Sample mission statements for not-for-profit organizations

Champions of Caring
Champions of Caring is a not-for-profit 501(c)(3) organization dedicated to sensitizing, educating, and empowering young people to take active roles in improving their communities. Our community and school-based programs help reduce prejudice, encourage service, and develop cultures of caring.

Red Cross
The American Red Cross, a humanitarian organization led by volunteers and guided by its Congressional Charter and the Fundamental Principles of the International Red Cross Movement, will provide relief to victims of disasters and help people prevent, prepare for, and respond to emergencies.

Greenpeace
Greenpeace is an independent campaigning organization that uses peaceful direct action and creative communication to expose global environmental problems, and to promote solutions that are essential to a peaceful and green future.

American Youth Understanding Diabetes Abroad (AYUDA)
AYUDA strives to raise awareness of, and promote, sustainable development for diabetes communities throughout the Americas by using youth as agents for change.

Write your own mission statement:

Step # 4: Identify Community Partners

You need other people in order to succeed. Begin to identify individuals or organizations that can be helpful to you.

For the Beginner:

- Whom can you recruit to join you?
- Friends?
- Family?
- Your children?
- Co-workers?
- Members of your religious community?

For the Intermediate or Advanced:

- Who is already in your network?
- Whom do you need to get involved? Involve people who you feel "get it" and are committed to your cause.

In addition to the above list, the following agencies can be helpful:

- Nonprofit agencies
- Your local, state, and federal government officials
- Government agencies
- Local businesses
- Colleges and universities
- Social organizations
- Religious organizations
- Media
- Corporations

Brainstorm ideas for community partners:

- Who would be interested in your mission?
- What is their interest?
- Why would they want to get involved?
- What could they contribute?

Script yourself:

Before each phone call or meeting, create a list of the important points that you want to make. Your last question should always be: "Do you know anyone else who might be interested in this project?"

My Community Partners

My Community Partner:	Resource They Can Provide:	Phone:	E-mail:	Address:
Action Taken:				

My Community Partner:	Resource They Can Provide:	Phone:	Email:	Address:
Action Taken:				

My Community Partner:	Resource They Can Provide:	Phone:	Email:	Address:
Action Taken:				

Step # 5: Create an Action Plan and Timeline

For the Beginner:

- Figure out your time commitment. Where and how does this fit into your schedule? *Don't overcommit.* You can always increase your involvement.
- Will you be involved daily, weekly, or monthly?

For the Intermediate:

- Stay organized. This is the key to a successful project. If you are working with a group, delegate tasks and keep a list of who is responsible for each part of the project.
- Which tasks need to be accomplished first?
- Are there several tasks that need to be worked on at the same time?
- If you are working with a group, how frequently will you need to be in touch or meet to get feedback about each person's progress?

For the Advanced:

- In addition to your timeline, you should create a strategic plan. Where do you see this project in the next three months, six months, year, or three years?
- Are there things that you need to do now to ensure that this endeavor is sustainable in the future?

Use the chart on the following page to organize your tasks by week and month. If you are able to commit to your project on a daily basis, create a more detailed daily calendar.

Break your timeline down by month, and then by week, to keep yourself on schedule!

	Tasks to be Completed This Week/ Month	Who Will Be Involved?	Outcomes	What Are My Next Steps?
Month				
Week 1				
Week 2				
Week 3				
Week 4				

Step #6: Develop a Budget and Fundraising Strategy

There is no magic formula for fundraising—however, having an itemized budget is *absolutely necessary*. Knowing your financial commitment to the project is vital.

For the Beginner:

- If your new activity involves serving on an advisory board, find out about the financial commitment. Many boards require a minimum annual donation from their members.
- If you are working with friends or family members, do you need money to fund the project?

For the Intermediate or Advanced:

- Create a budget.
- Do you need start-up funds?
- Where will the funds come from?
- Identify funders with whom your mission will resonate. Find out if your local library has a grants department where you can do your research. Look at the mission statements of corporations and foundations to see if your project matches up with their interests.
- Think of creative ways to raise funds. How can you turn social events and activities into fundraising opportunities? Remember how Alison turned dinner parties into an opportunity to raise funds and collect books. Or, how Christine organized a gala to raise funds and awareness about her mission. Consider the costs and potential revenue of each type of fundraiser.
- Asking for in-kind donations of goods or services is another option. Remember, *pro bono!* "Free" is the best word in any language.

Step #7: Spread the Word

Someone once said to me, "If I don't read about you in a newspaper, or see you on TV, or the Internet, then you don't exist." It was a harsh thing to say, but I understood the sentiment. Notify local media outlets of upcoming events by using press releases and media advisories. Make a video about your project to publicize it, or create your own Web site.

For the Beginner:

- E-mail your friends, family, or associates about what you are doing.
- Start a blog. Keep people informed about your progress and share your reflections. It might inspire them to join you, or make a financial or in-kind contribution to the project or organization.

For the Intermediate or Advanced:

- The more that people know about what you are doing, the better. You never know where the next great idea might come from, or who can provide a resource. Get your name and your mission out there in creative ways.
- Create a Web site, blog, or a profile for a social networking site, such as Facebook or LinkedIn.
- Write an article for your local newspaper or magazine, or try to get interviewed by a television or radio station.
- Speak at your church, synagogue, mosque, or other local organizations.

Step # 8: Evaluate Your Progress

If things aren't going right, don't keep spinning your wheels. Evaluate and modify your plans on a regular basis. Furthermore, you should review and modify your plans even if things are going well. You might find that you want to increase your involvement.

For the Beginner:

- If things are going well, discuss taking on more responsibilities, or expanding your project.
- If you are not happy with your involvement, uncomfortable with your group, or you feel that your ideas and work are not valued, look for another organization or other people to get involved with. Tweak your ideas, and create a back-up plan.

For the Intermediate or Advanced:

Get input from others. *Don't be defensive.* If all of the pieces of your project aren't coming together, that doesn't mean it can't work. Ask yourself:

- Where have I had success?
- Where am I wasting energy?
- Should I change the direction of the work that I am doing?
- Is there a more pressing authentic need that must be addressed first?
- Are there other people that I need to get involved? Are there resources or skills that I am lacking to complete this project?

Step #9: Reflect

Reflect upon how this project has impacted your life and the lives of others. If you enjoy keeping a journal, record your successes and failures, and ask yourself:

- What have I learned?
- What successes have I had?
- What would I have done differently?
- How has my involvement in this project changed me?
- How has it impacted others?
- What lessons do I want to share with others?
- What has this project added to my life?
- What gift am I leaving to the future?
- What is the legacy that I am creating by doing this work?

Get testimonials from those who participated or benefited from your project.

This is also a good place to record ideas you might have for growing and sustaining the project.

Step #10: Celebrate and Promote Your Successes

I have sometimes been criticized for recognizing and honoring students for doing service. I've heard the argument that service should be selfless, and that one should not seek recognition for doing good. I agree with the philosopher Maimonides who said that the highest level of service is performed anonymously. However, I have also learned through Champions of Caring that an effective way to inspire others to get involved is to *show* them the good that you are doing—to be a role model. By being recognized, you motivate others to serve.

It is also important to celebrate your accomplishments with others in your community. It gives those involved a feeling of success and a sense of pride in what they have done:

- Have a party.
- Honor those who have helped you. If people can't attend, *always* send thank-you notes.
- Put your accomplishments in a newsletter, Web site, or blog. You never know what resources may come along for your project by highlighting your work through the media, and recruiting others to help you.

As I said at the beginning, creating a legacy is both selfless and selfish. Feel good about living your legacy. Making legacy-building fun and engaging keeps people involved and helps ensure that they will come back and share their experiences with others.

Now that you have created your project, remember that sustainability is key. If the project is making an impact, it should be well documented so that others can replicate it and further develop it. Never keep everything in your head. Living a legacy is about creating and sharing something that is sustainable.

How to Use the Ten Steps to Create a Project

You may still be thinking, "How do I really do this?" On the following pages, I have provided an example of how you can work through the steps to create a project at the Intermediate level. This example is based on having about five hours per week to spend on the project. Following that, there is a guide for taking the next step and creating your own not-for-profit.

Step #1: Identify an Authentic Need

Need	Evidence of need	What is being done to address this need?	How can I get involved with these efforts?	How can I add value to what is currently being done?
Hunger	There are a lot of homeless people asking for money for food outside of my local grocery store.	There are Federal food stamp programs that help, but they are not sufficient.	I can participate in a food drive for the homeless shelter and encourage my friends and family to participate.	I can use my personal network and skills to support the existing organizations in the community and help them to get more resources.
	I recently read an article in the newspaper about a local soup kitchen that does not have enough funding to meet the needs of the people in the community.	There are two homeless shelters in the community, but they cannot serve everyone in need.	I can volunteer to serve meals at the homeless shelters.	
	I went online and found that my city has very high statistics for families who run out of food stamps before the end of the month.	Local faith-based communities organize food drives, but usually only around the holidays.		
		There are free lunch programs in schools, but the food is not nutritious.		

Step #2: Choose Your Project.

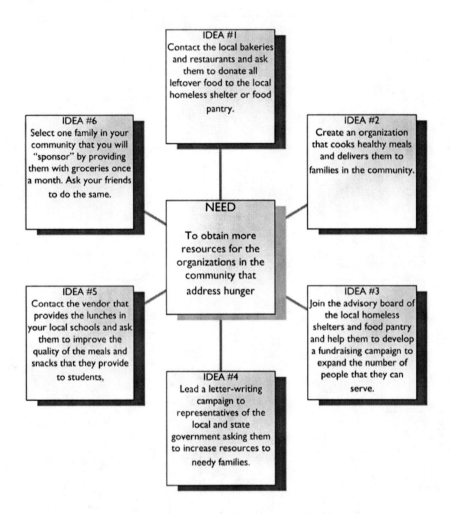

IDEA #1
Contact the local bakeries and restaurants and ask them to donate all leftover food to the local homeless shelter or food pantry.

IDEA #6
Select one family in your community that you will "sponsor" by providing them with groceries once a month. Ask your friends to do the same.

IDEA #2
Create an organization that cooks healthy meals and delivers them to families in the community.

NEED
To obtain more resources for the organizations in the community that address hunger

IDEA #5
Contact the vendor that provides the lunches in your local schools and ask them to improve the quality of the meals and snacks that they provide to students,

IDEA #3
Join the advisory board of the local homeless shelters and food pantry and help them to develop a fundraising campaign to expand the number of people that they can serve.

IDEA #4
Lead a letter-writing campaign to representatives of the local and state government asking them to increase resources to needy families.

Evaluation of my ideas:

Idea #1: I really like this idea and already have a lot of connections to bakeries and restaurants in my own social network. However, the challenge will be transporting the food from restaurants and bakeries to the homeless shelters. My car is not large enough, but maybe I can find some partners to help me.

Idea #2: I don't really have the time or space to prepare meals in large quantities at this point, but I might want to work toward this goal in the future.

Idea #3: My experience in fundraising and development makes this idea very appealing. However, I feel like I want to do something completely different from my job, and develop some new skills sets.

Idea #4: This is too "hands-off." I want to work more at the grassroots level.

Idea #5: I know that often parents sacrifice for their children. I want to help entire families, not just the students who are in school.

Idea #6: Again, I really like this idea, but would need help in identifying a family. I'd also like to make a greater impact.

After reviewing these six ideas, I decided that Idea #1 was the best choice. It highlights my skills, utilizes my community connections, and is hands-on. The time commitment will match the amount of time that I am willing to commit to this project. Although transportation is an obstacle, I feel confident that I can engage a community partner to help. Before entering into this project, I will have to check with these institutions to make sure that they will accept my donations.

Step #3: Mission Statement for Idea #1

My mission is to empower the local homeless shelters and food bank to serve more families and individuals by organizing donations from local restaurants and community partners. My goal is to collect and transport excess food and supplies that are otherwise discarded by these community partners, and to deliver them to these needy organizations for distribution.

Step #4: Identify community partners

- I have to find a location to store and distribute all of the food that is collected for the local homeless shelters and food pantry.
- I know that Joe's Bakery throws away all leftover bread, sandwiches, and desserts at the end of the day on Sunday. The owner agreed that I can have all of the leftover food if I find a way to collect and transport it.
- The supermarket where I shop agreed to donate milk and juice to accompany the food that the bakery is donating.
- The local high school is a good resource. The basketball team has a van that I can utilize to transport the food. The players are required to do community service, and will assist with the pickup and delivery.
- A culinary arts program at the high school, where the students cook large quantities of food, has agreed to donate prepared meals to the shelter.

Step #5: Create an Action Plan and Timeline

Month	Tasks to be completed this month	Who will be involved?	Outcomes	What are my next steps?
September	Get all of my community partners to agree about their respective roles and responsibilities.	Each of my community partners: the shelters, bakery, supermarket, and high school.	Created a task list of individuals who would be responsible for each aspect of the project.	Create and distribute a schedule for pickup and delivery.
October	Organize and implement our first four weekly food pickups and deliveries. Evaluate each pickup and delivery.	Each of my community partners.	Each of the four pickups and deliveries were accomplished on schedule.	Get feedback from each of my partners.
November	Continue weekly food pickups and delivery. Contact the local newspaper and ask them to write a story about the project as a way to attract funders.	Each of my community partners.	Food deliveries continue, but we are not getting the press coverage or funding attention that we need.	Find a public relations expert who will publicize this work *pro bono*.

Step #5: Create an Action Plan and Timeline

Month	Tasks to be completed this month	Who will be involved?	Outcomes	What are my next steps?
December	Continue weekly food pickups and deliveries. Begin to work on designing a fundraising campaign and/or seek sponsors to donate fresh fruits and vegetables. Find out what steps I have to take to collect funds for the shelter. Establish a bank account for the funds we raise.	Each of my community partners. Friends who have experiences with fundraising for other organizations. Legal and accounting partners.	Deliveries continue. Researched the steps that I need to take to collect funds Established a bank account.	Begin the plans for a community garden. Find partners who can assist with fundraising, accounting and legal issues as they arise.

Step #6: Outline Your Financial Commitment

Because I am focusing on redistributing existing resources, the only real cost at this point is gas for the van to transport the items. I am able to pay for this out-of-pocket until I can find a sponsor.

Step #7: Spread the Word

I will talk to my family members and friends about what I am doing, and ask them if they know of any other resources in the community. I will also reach out to the local media to do a story.

Step #8: Evaluate Your Project

The food pickups and deliveries are a success. However, the food that is donated is not always the most nutritious. There is definitely still a need for fresh fruits and vegetables. My next step is to begin to raise funds for this project that will enable us to purchase fresher foods. A longer-term goal for the spring is to plant a community garden at the shelter.

Step #9: Reflect

I feel that I have not only been able to provide food and resources to the shelters, but by getting the local high school students involved, I have mentored the next generation to get involved in service as well.

Step #10: Celebrate and Promote Your Successes

I will invite all of my community partners to celebrate our accomplishments in an event held at one of the shelters. They will be asked to help serve a meal, and will be recognized with certificates of appreciation. Or, I might have a community celebration once we have planted our community garden, and again, invite the media to cover this event to gain even more exposure and support.

CHAPTER 7. THE NEXT LEVEL: TIPS FOR BECOMING A SOCIAL ENTREPRENEUR

Social entrepreneurship is a growing movement. My story of becoming a social entrepreneur and creating Champions of Caring is one of many. Individuals and groups are using their skills and innovations to become change agents for society. Around the globe, social entrepreneurs are addressing our most pressing social issues, such as education, healthcare, hunger, and economic development. Before deciding if you are ready to take on the challenge of creating an organization or project at an advanced level, explore the following Web sites to learn more about social entrepreneurship and what others are doing in the field:

- The Skoll Foundation, (skollfoundation.org) provides research on social entrepreneurship and profiles of social entrepreneurs.
- The Schwab Foundation for Social Entrepreneurship (schwabfound.org) allows you to search for social entrepreneurs by categories such as name, organization, area of impact, and organizational model.
- Ashoka, (ashoka.org) is the global association of social entrepreneurs, allowing you to build your own network by connecting with others.

- The New Heroes project, sponsored by PBS (pbs.org/opb/thenewheroes) shares dramatic stories of social entrepreneurs from around the world, and offers resources to parents and educators to share these stories with youth.
- *How to Change the World: Social Entrepreneurs and the Power of New Ideas* by David Bornstein is a powerful book that shares the stories of social entrepreneurs and provides additional resources for people who want to become social entrepreneurs.

Are You Ready to Become a Social Entrepreneur?

So how do you know if you are ready to become a social entrepreneur and start your own not-for-profit organization? Before I started Champions of Caring, I did my research, and realized that there was no other organization doing the scope of work that I was proposing. I then asked myself several questions which I now recommend that you reflect on:

- What is my motivation for starting a not-for-profit?
- What cause or issue will I address?
- What is my mission statement?
- What is the value added of creating this organization? Whom will it benefit?
- Whose help will I need to implement my project?
- Do I have the skills, time, energy, and financial resources necessary to succeed?
- How will I measure if I am successful?

Although I felt that I was in a good position to start Champions of Caring, I realized that my fundraising and technology skills were not what they needed to be, but I did not let that stop me from going forward. I knew that I could take courses to improve these skills, and find people who were more knowledgeable in these areas to help me. I did not have all of the programmatic pieces in place, but that didn't stop me either. I knew that over time, and with the help of others, I would be able to develop the necessary programs. I had the motivation, the mission, resources, time, and energy to proceed. If you have answered these questions and feel comfortable to go forward, the next section provides some general tips for getting started.

Starting a Not-for-Profit Organization

Starting a not-for-profit is a challenging but rewarding endeavor. There are volumes written on how to create a not-for-profit, but I want to share some suggestions based upon my own experiences.

- Keep in mind that there are many rules and regulations that govern the operation of a nonprofit organization, depending upon the state in which you live. This may include a yearly audit, or filing tax forms to special reporting agencies. Surprisingly, there is usually more administrative paperwork necessary to operate a charitable organization than a for-profit business.
- Be ready to define your charitable purpose. (That's where the mission statement you created earlier becomes very important.)
- Check with your state's office of business or economic development to determine their requirements for creating a not-for-profit organization.
- Check with the local IRS office to find out the necessary forms to file.
- Consult an attorney and accountant for guidance.
- Depending on organizing requirements, you may need to develop a set of bylaws to guide the operations of your organization, and a set of articles of incorporation.

The bylaws are *extremely important*. They should provide instructions regarding the selection and responsibilities of board members and other personnel, as well as information about insurance as it relates to the operation of your non-profit. Having all of this information clearly defined also helps with sustainability of the organization. The articles of incorporation name the entity, its location, the organizing purposes, and potential liabilities.

Creating a Logo and Branding

As you begin your organization, think about the image that you want to project. It is important to be consistent with your logo and branding, just as you would if starting a business. Your logo and brand should be easily recognizable.

- Stay true to your mission statement while creating your logo. Try to scale it down to one sentence, or phrase, for your logo.
- Look at the logos of other nonprofits that are addressing similar issues. Do they use traditional fonts and images, or creative fonts and flashy graphics? Think about how you want to differentiate your logo from others.
- Focus on your message. Decide what you want to communicate about your organization. Who are your target audiences? These elements should play an important role in the overall design.
- Make your logo clean and functional. Your logo should look as good on a business card as it does on letterhead, or t-shirts. It should be easy to reproduce, memorable, and distinctive. Be sure to create a logo that can be reproduced in black and white so that it can be faxed, photocopied, or used in a black-and-white ad as effectively as in color.
- Limit your words. The best logos make an *immediate statement* with a picture or illustration—not just words.
- Hire a designer if possible. If you can't afford a designer, turn to your local art schools and try to find a student intern.
- Protect your logo. Once you've produced a logo that embodies your organization's mission at a glance, make sure you trademark it to protect it from use by other companies. You can apply for a trademark through the U.S. Patent and Trademark Office (uspto.gov).
- Use your logo everywhere you can: on business cards, stationery, letterhead, brochures, ads, your Web

sites, and any other place where you mention your organization's name.

Establishing a Board

As I've stressed throughout this book, you need *people* to make your vision a success. An active, well-connected board is invaluable.

- Look for people who care about your mission *and* are active. It helps to have members with different skills such as law, public relations, and accounting.
- Be clear about the commitment that is required.
- Outline the responsibilities of the board. These may include providing networking and funding opportunities, evaluating the financial health of the organization, and participating in strategic planning and making a financial commitment.
- Keep your board members updated on a regular basis.

Fundraising

In a perfect world, funding would not be such a difficult issue, and not-for-profit organizations could focus on creating and delivering quality programs. Fundraising takes time, perseverance, and creativity. There are many approaches to fundraising, and you will find a combination of methods that work for you.

- Conduct research about grants online, or at your local library. Look for foundation grants that have guidelines that are similar to your mission statement and goals. If you can hire a professional grant writer, do so, but keep in mind that you know your mission and goals better than anyone. If you cannot hire a grant writer, it might be helpful to find someone with grant-writing experience to initially guide you through the process and evaluate the grants you have written.

- Look for corporations with offices or factories in your area, local foundations, or philanthropists who you think will support your mission.
- When at all possible, organize face-to-face meetings to familiarize people with your cause. Ask friends, board members, and supporters to host events in their homes or offices. Introduce people to your cause and build support before asking for money.
- Experiment with online fundraising tools, such as Firstgiving (firstgiving.com). Keep track of every donation, no matter how small. Track your donors, and *always* send personalized thank-you notes. This is how you build relationships with repeat donors. Don't forget to keep track of *pro bono* services or in-kind donations. You need this information for personal records, and for the IRS.

Tips for Making Your Organization a Success

- **Be open to opportunities, but stay true to your mission**. I never expected to bring Champions of Caring to South Africa. However, it was an opportunity that was in line with my mission of empowering young people to change their communities. I have had opportunities in the past that I had to turn down. Although they were wonderful connections, they were not aligned with what I really wanted to accomplish. Stay focused on your mission. As my friend Patti says, "Diversify but don't 'di-worsify'."
- **Be professional**. Even if you are working out of your home, create a home office space. Get a separate phone line, set up separate e-mail accounts, and create letterhead and envelopes with your logo.
- **Be professional, part II**. In a world of Blackberries, wireless Internet, cell phones, and blogging, you can be in touch almost anywhere at anytime. If you are still working full-time, respond to people in a timely

manner. You never know when you might get an e-mail from someone who could really support your cause.

- **Be visible.** Go to events that can help you to network and further your cause.

- **Talk it up.** Remember that you are not promoting yourself; you are promoting your cause. This will give you the moxy and incentive to do the work. If you care enough about your cause, you can get over your self-consciousness. When you see people who can further your cause, *reach out to them.* Keep it short and don't tell them your life story—just have your key points ready.

- **Try not to be overbearing.** Use tact if someone is just not ready to listen. Don't overwhelm people with your enthusiasm and take up too much of their time.

- **When describing your work, stay true to your mission.** Focus on the pieces of your story that will most resonate with the person you are talking to, and tie it into that person's interests to gain his or her support.

- **If you are asking for help, be clear about what you need.** Sometimes people don't realize how they can help.

- **Interns, interns, interns!** On a tight budget, it is often difficult to get help. Over the years, we have recruited wonderful high school and college students, and retired individuals to make phone calls, stuff envelopes, and help us to get organized for events. While we have used traditional methods, like recruiting through local colleges and universities, two of our interns have been lifeguards at the pool where I was doing rehab for a back injury! After chatting for a while, I saw that they were energetic and interested. So, shamelessly, while in a bathing suit and swimming laps, I asked them to volunteer. They have been wonderful assets to my organization!

- **Don't count your chickens before they are hatched.** Be sure that you have the support, or money promised, before you move forward and make commitments.
- **Take rejection in stride.** I once got a rejection letter for a grant request, stating that they would not support us because we did not raise enough money that year. Even with years of success, we happened to have some financial difficulties at the time. The kicker was that this was a funder who had supported us in the past, and claimed to love our program. This only reinforced my resolve, and fueled me to work even harder and smarter.
- **Always carry a business card.** Even on vacation— you just never know. (Remember the unexpected opportunity I had in South Africa!)
- **Always be prepared to quietly and respectfully pounce.** In a department store, I once solicited a donation from a man I knew while he was trying on shoes. As he was saying, "Barb you are too much," he was also writing me a check! Again, not for me— but for *my cause*. Be careful, because this could easily annoy someone. You always must know whom you are approaching, and have a strong sense of how the person will react.
- **Pilot programs and get feedback from the experts.** Start small and see how things work. Learn from your mistakes. We continually update our curriculum and programs based upon student and teacher input.
- **Collect data.** This can include statistics or qualitative data such as interviews and testimonials from the people who benefit from your service. This sets you apart from others, and will help you to make a credible case to funding sources.
- **Surround yourself with people who are smarter and more organized than you.** Having a strong team keeps you focused and will help ensure success.

- **Find people who complement your skills.** If you are a public relations professional who is great with people but struggles with organization, find an administrative partner.
- **Learn from others and build on it.** Do your research. If there are other organizations doing similar work, what are you going to do that's different? If your idea has already been put into action by someone else, collaborate— *don't replicate.*
- **Stay away from naysayers.** Surround yourself with positive people, and avoid the "toxic" ones.
- **Choose what you ask for carefully.** Think big, and think *strategically.* Before you ask for assistance, prioritize your needs. Then, consider if there is something bigger or more important you might need to ask this person or organization for in the future.
- **Always have a plan B, C, and D.**

Chapter 8. MAKE YOUR LEGACY AN INTERGENERATIONAL AND FAMILY AFFAIR

The most important part of living your legacy is sharing it with others. The final two chapters will help you to find ways to share your legacy with your children, grandchildren, family, and friends through meaningful intergenerational projects, and by composing Legacy Letters, and creating Legacy Clubs.

Teach Our Children Well

You've got to be taught before it's too late
Before you are six or seven or eight
To hate all the people your relatives hate,
You have to be carefully taught.
—Oscar Hammerstein, lyricist and playwright

These lyrics powerfully demonstrate the importance of how we as a society raise our children, and the impact of the values we teach them. Now, more than ever, whatever your religion or culture, there can be no more valuable legacy than to raise the next generation of youth to become caring, compassionate, and responsible citizens. In recounting her experiences at the hands of her captors, my mother never fails to remind me that millions died in a master plan devised by the intelligentsia of German society. "A head without a heart is dangerous," she warns.

Whether you are a parent, grandparent, aunt, uncle, teacher, mentor, or just someone who cares about the next generation, teaching our children to care is both a privilege and responsibility. In this day and age, nothing is business-as-usual— not even *parenting*. In some parts of the world, children fulfill the legacy of their parents by sacrificing their own lives in missions of hate disguised as justice. If people are actively teaching children hatred, then we must respond by raising an army of compassionate people. We must equip them with the skills and tools to combat injustice wherever they see it—in the classroom, on the streets—anywhere people are powerless to defend themselves. My mother says that the best defense is love. Once liberated from the death camps, my parents didn't seek revenge. They rebuilt their lives and had children. They would not give their tormentors the satisfaction of ruining their futures, as well. Fighting hate with love is a powerful tool.

Carpe Diem

> *"Children have never been very good at listening to their elders, but they have never failed to imitate them."*
> —James Baldwin, writer and civil rights activist

We don't typically use the word "character" to describe a six-year-old. But at what age is it apparent that a child possesses qualities of character? Or does not? At what point do you say, "Oh, darn, I forgot to teach them character"? Twelve? Twenty? Babies aren't born having an opinion about anything at all. They're a *tabula rasa*, just waiting for input from us.

With the laudable goal of wanting our children to thrive in a competitive society, we push to develop them academically, athletically, even musically. But so often along the way, we forget to develop their hearts. Why not include character-building with the rest of our parental responsibilities, such as making sure their teeth are straight and their homework is done? As parents and concerned citizens, we know that if the next generation is to reach its potential to improve our society, we have to participate *actively* in the learning process.

It is as true as it is cliché: Children learn by example. As my mother says, "If you don't do it, don't say it." We must teach compassion by showing it. We have to take advantage of every opportunity to discuss values, ethics, and making wise choices with our children—from childhood, throughout adulthood. With young children, encourage them when they show character. Many families create reward charts for completing chores where their children are incentivized for completing household tasks. Some children are even given money, or a gift, for achieving good grades. Why not create a "Character Chart" as well? Reward children for being kind to their siblings, resolving conflicts, helping without being asked, saying *please* and *thank you*, or calling or visiting their grandparents. Character doesn't just happen. It needs to be modeled, reinforced, and *rewarded*. We have to engage our children in conversation and have real dialogues about moral dilemmas so that when they are faced with a problem they're comfortable coming to us for advice.

Give Them Roots

It is important that we help young people understand where they came from, and to feel that they are a part of a legacy bigger than themselves. As I have shared throughout this book, my family history and the values and lessons my parents instilled in me from a young age are the driving forces in my life. They have guided all of my decisions and made me the person I am.

Think about the people and events in your family history that have influenced you. Have you done enough to share this information with the next generation? You never know what aspect of your family's history will spark their interest. Maybe there was an event or a tragedy in your family that will motivate them to take action. They may also be inspired by the heroic and courageous actions of members of your family, and feel driven to make their own mark.

Don't wait to share your family history with your children. If you are lucky to have elderly relatives who are still living, record or videotape oral histories. Have them explain the context of family photos, and describe the characteristics and values of other family members. If this isn't possible, do a research project to find out about your family's background. Or take a trip with your family to trace their roots and learn firsthand about their lives. This is a great way to discuss what your family stands for, and to pass on values from one generation to the next.

Make Your Own Traditions

In our busy, frenetic lives, simply finding time to be with your family is a true challenge; let alone finding time to do service. Don't separate the two. Like so many endeavors, the process can begin at home. Home is our center, and often a source of strength. Begin at home.

Some families have regular meetings to discuss everything from schedule conflicts to moral and ethical dilemmas. One family I know has mandatory Sunday dinners where each family member has the floor for at least ten minutes, rebuttals optional. Another family calls meetings to make major decisions. In this way, everyone is heard, whether his or her suggestion is acted upon or not. At the very least, this exercise teaches that it's important to allow individuals to have their say. *Everyone's* voice matters.

Doing Service as a Family

And while we're at it, why not think of ways for the family to be together in service to others? Is there someone in town who has suffered a fire, death, or other traumatic event and could use some help? Maybe you could make a meal and deliver it to them while they heal. Or, perhaps you could mow their lawn, take out their trash, or run errands for them. Your example as parents, neighbors, and friends could make a lasting impression on your children about what it means to belong to a community—to *demonstrate* caring and respect for others.

Do service as a family, but be sure to pick something your kids will enjoy. The ideas should always come from *them*. You can encourage and guide them, but try to find something that they really care about. One of the biggest mistakes made in introducing children to service is to force them to do something that they are not interested in. When I was in high school, I had to do community service. It was mandatory to become a candy-striper and help out at the local hospital. I was scared to death of hospitals, and the thought of visiting one on a weekly basis frightened me. I remember begging my mother to write a note to get me out of this service project. This was not a good introduction to doing service.

Many of the teens that I have worked with say that it was their parents and family members who showed them the connection between character and service. As one Champion, Hope, explains, her father introduced her to service, and continued to lead service trips for her and her peers throughout high school: "Throughout my childhood, my dad often asked 'How's your heart?' Although I still have trouble expressing an answer, at least I have come to understand the question. I find my heart in serving and loving others."

Karen, another Champion, explains, "As far back as I can remember, my parents have instilled in me the value of giving back to the community. My parents have taught me through their own lives. I also have four younger sisters who are always looking to me as an example. I feel that by having them see my love for service, it will inspire them to follow and be involved in service themselves."

For the Record: Not a Body of Work, a Body of *Life*

Creating family traditions is a marvelous legacy-building activity. So is documenting those traditions. Many school districts across the country have popularized the practice of building educational portfolios for each student. From the time a child enters kindergarten or first grade, samples of his or her work from each year are added to the portfolio. Upon graduation from high school, the student is given the portfolio, which serves as an irreplaceable body of work chronicling their evolution from crayons to chemistry.

Why not bring the educational portfolio concept home by helping children develop legacy portfolios demonstrating what their family stands for? Whenever the family participates in any selfless act, document it as you would any other special event such as a birthday party or a graduation ceremony. Annual action plans can also make their way into the legacy portfolios. Add newspaper clippings, powerful quotes, and magazine articles that helped motivate or inspire a family member along the way. And by all means, add notes of more personal accomplishments illustrating moments of compassion and inspiration that contributed to your children's character development. The impact of a legacy portfolio on a child can be profound. It is not a body of work, but a body of *life*. It is a keepsake that inspires and reminds children to reflect on their values and how they lead their lives. But more significantly, it need never stop growing, and it can be passed on to the next generation.

Building character and doing service as a family from childhood through the teenage years allows our children to find what they are passionate about. It is also a way to stay connected and involved in your children's lives during the tumultuous adolescent years.

Here are some ideas to help your child get involved in improving his or her community, and the world:

- Help them to get inspired by sharing the stories of Champions that I have included in this book. They are proof that young people really can make a difference in the world!
- Have them search the Internet for stories about how young people are giving back, and examples of service projects. A Web site called "What Kids Can Do" (whatkidscando.org) includes inspiring stories and first person accounts of young volunteers and their experiences with service.
- Introduce them to the political process at a young age. The Web site servicevote.org is a great site that introduces young people to civic participation.

149

- Visit the "Parent's Resource" page of the National Service Learning Clearinghouse Web site (servicelearning.org), or Learn to Give (learningtogive.org) for ideas about projects that you can do together.
- Ask them to look within their own school. Are there issues they want to change? Is there bullying? Lack of respect? Prejudice against different groups?
- Have a family discussion about getting involved in service.
- Encourage your children to talk to their friends about issues that concern them in the community, or the world.
- Help your children use their talents and activities to make a difference. If they are athletes, encourage them to teach their sports skills to a younger child, or get the members of their teams to do service together. Are your children involved in music or theater? Maybe they can provide performances for the residents of senior centers, put together a play, or write music that deals with ethical dilemmas, to present at a school assembly.
- Encourage your children to work with their church, synagogue, or mosque group; or create an interfaith project.
- Support them in creating a Bar/Bat Mitzvah or confirmation project.
- Encourage your children to become a mentor for a younger student.
- Create a Champions of Caring Club at their school. Talk to teachers and administrators. For information about creating a club, go to championsofcaring.org.
- E-mail me at Champions of Caring (Barbara@ championsofcaring.org) for more ideas about how to get started!

Chapter 9: REACHING OUT: LEGACY LETTERS AND LEGACY CLUBS

Composing Legacy Letters

As you begin to live your legacy, I encourage you to start to share what you have learned about yourself with others. A special gift to your family members, friends, and colleagues is to write a Legacy Letter. This is a document which tells the reader who you are, what you are passionate about, and how you have lived your legacy. It can also include elements of your family history, important life experiences that you have shared, and life lessons that you've learned. Sharing this letter with loved ones opens the opportunity for discussion and enriches existing relationships. It might even encourage them to think about the values that you have in common—and in so doing, to find their own passion and live their own legacy.

I also encourage you to write these letters to the people who have influenced or mentored you throughout your life. In my life, my mother and John Crystal were two major influences. Who has influenced your life? Who has been your mentor? Write to them and tell them the impact they have made on your life. If that person has passed away, this is still an insightful personal exercise to help you to understand how their influence shaped who you are today.

Many people wait until they are older and writing their wills to think about writing Legacy Letters. I encourage you to start *now*. These letters can become a family tradition, to be exchanged on birthdays, anniversaries, or special occasions. You can update these letters every year. Legacy Letters offer a unique opportunity to share your values and stay connected to people in a very meaningful way.

The format can be whatever you wish. It may be one page, or twenty pages. You could even record it on a CD, or create a slideshow. In fact, I consider this book my legacy letter to my family and friends.

Composing a Legacy Letter

In writing your letter, here are some important questions to help guide you:

To whom will you write your Legacy Letter?

- Is there someone who has been influential in your life that you would like to express your gratitude to?
- Are there family members (children, grandchildren, or nieces and nephews) whom you want to share your family history and core values with?
- Is there a person in your life whom you want to inspire by your example?
- Will this letter be specifically addressed to one person, or will it be a general letter that could be shared with multiple people in your life?

What details will you include about yourself in this letter?

- Your family history and lessons that you learned from your family.
- A childhood dream that you pursued, or would still like to pursue.
- The values that are most important to you.
- Your greatest accomplishment(s).
- Your interests.

- The causes or issues you were most passionate about, and what you did to address them.
- An experience that you shared with them that was meaningful to you.
- What you appreciate or admire most about them.
- Your hopes for their future.

What form will your Legacy Letter take?

- A letter or series of letters.
- An audio recording.
- A video.
- An autobiographical sketch.
- Poetry.
- A photo album.
- A portfolio that combines several of these elements.

Starting a Legacy Club

Whether you are at a Beginner, Intermediate, or Advanced level, living your legacy should be *enjoyable*. It should be an opportunity to share your passion and energy with others. I suggest starting a Legacy Club—a group of people (family, friends, colleagues) who come together and use their collective skills and resources to address an issue—as a great way to gain support for your projects and inspire others to begin to live their legacies. Just as I hope that my story motivated you to get started, you can do the same for others.

Begin by pulling together friends, family members, colleagues, or neighbors. Share the concept of Legacy Clubs and living your legacy with them. If you already have an idea for a project, present it to the group. Ask for their input and suggestions about your project, and discuss the various ways they might get involved and support this project.

If you are still not clear about what issues you want to address, starting a Legacy Club is a good forum for brainstorming potential causes. Your fellow club members might know about issues in your community that you were not aware of. Or, they might have a cause that is important to them.

Most likely, not everyone whom you invite to join your Legacy Club will be as passionate about the same cause as you. That's okay. You might inspire them to find a cause of their own, and then come together to share strategies. Or, they may be willing to share a skill to empower you to achieve your goals.

If you like the concept of working on projects as a group, but are not interested in the same cause, you might want to take turns every few months choosing a new cause or project, or doing individual projects around a theme. You might start with one project, and then branch off into smaller groups who address different facets of the project. For example, one group or committee might focus on public relations, while another might focus on fundraising.

Legacy Club Guide

Use the questions below to help guide your Legacy Club.

Before you get started:

What topic do you want to address in your Legacy Club?

Whom will you invite to be a part of your Legacy Club?

When, where and how frequently will you meet?

In your first meeting, discuss the following questions:

What are the goals of each of the members of your Legacy Club? What does each member hope to get out of this club?

Will club members focus on one project topic, or will you address different topics?

Share your Legacy Profiles. What are the talents, skills and resources that each person in your Legacy Club brings to the group? What can each member contribute?

How much time can each member commit?

What other skills will you need to be successful? Who in your organization or community might have these skills?

In each meeting, also reflect on the following questions:

Discussion Topics for Your Legacy Club:

- What issue or cause am I passionate about?
- What aspect of this issue do I want to address?
- What skills are needed to be successful?
- What impact have my efforts made on the cause being addressed?
- What have I contributed to the success of the project?
- What has worked well?
- What has not worked well?
- What needs to be changed?

- How has my work contributed to creating a culture of caring?
- What about my involvement in the Legacy Club makes me proudest?
- How has living my legacy impacted me? How have I grown as a person?
- How has the group been impacted by this club?
- What has been added to my life? New friends? New connections?
- Whom have I involved in living my legacy? How has this impacted them?
- What are my next steps to continue to live my legacy?

Join Our Legacy Clubs

Whether you have started your own Legacy Club or are working on your own project, *I want to hear from you*. I intend to make this book the first in a series, and hope to create future editions that share the accomplishments of its readers. I invite you to send your stories to me via e-mail (stories@embrace-your-legacy.com), or by using the form at the end of this book.

My goal is to create a Web site that will become a clearinghouse of ideas and resources, evolving into a worldwide network of people helping people. It will be a resource and idea bank with an interactive forum for creative exchange. That is how we will become an army of compassionate people leaving footprints and blueprints for future generations.

I know that even if you start by pursuing a solitary personal passion, you will no doubt want and need to share it at some point when it becomes bigger than you are. Everyone can benefit from sharing ideas with diversely talented and skilled people.

Your legacy will be enriched by sharing it with others who can help you take it to higher levels, and continue its momentum beyond your own involvement to create a stronger, more holistic outcome. And wouldn't that be amazing?

So what are you waiting for? Live your legacy now and share what you are doing with us. Whether you are in Philadelphia, Cape Town, Berlin, Peoria or Hawaii—*let's work together and change the world!*

LEGACY SUBMISSION FORM
Share your story with us.

Name:

Address:

Email: **Phone:**

Life Stage (Circle one):

  Youth   Young Professional   Baby Boomer   Retiree   Other:

What have you done to live your legacy now? Describe your project. Include your mission statement and goals.

Describe the impact that this project has had, or is having, on you and your community.

Optional Questions:

With whom are you working?

What are three things that you have learned about yourself through this project?

What new leadership skills have you gained?

How have you changed or grown through this project?

Other comments:

I hereby give Live Your Legacy Enterprises permission to use my stories, project descriptions, photographs and personal reflections on their websites, books, and promotional materials:

Signature: _____   **Date:** _____

☐ I would like to collaborate with others in the *Live Your Legacy Now* Community.
☐ I would like to receive information about Barbara Shaiman's *Embrace Your Legacy* speeches and workshops.

Please return this form by mail to: Live Your Legacy Enterprises, PO Box 568, Bala Cynwyd, PA 19004 or email your responses to stories@embrace-your-legacy.com. You can also submit the form via our website, www.embrace-your-legacy.com

Reflecting on Your Progress

Every night, before I go to bed, I take a minute to reflect upon how I lived my legacy throughout that day. What did I do to help others? What did I accomplish? What do I want to focus on tomorrow? I find that this is a very helpful exercise and it doesn't take much time.

As you embark on this journey of living your legacy, take the time to reflect on what you have accomplished, and where you are *heading*. It is important for you to evaluate and reflect upon the progress of your project, but it is also necessary to look at your life as a whole. After you get started, ask yourself the following questions on a daily, weekly, or monthly basis:

- Have I found my passion?
- Am I taking action to address a cause that I care about?
- How has living my legacy impacted me? How have I grown as a person?
- What has been added to my life? What has brought me the greatest fulfillment?
- Whom have I involved in living my legacy? How has this impacted them?
- What are my next steps to continue to live my legacy?

AFTERWORD

I started Champions of Caring in honor of my parents, but I continue to do the work for my children, grandchildren, and future generations. I want them to understand the importance of being Champions, and to inspire them to do good work and contribute to a kinder, more caring world.

Since I began writing this book, I have encountered great personal loss. My father died in November of 2008, at the age of eighty-nine. My mother, who is suffering from dementia, does not realize he is gone. In moments of lucidity, she still talks about the lessons she learned from being a Holocaust survivor. I frequently tell her about the accomplishments that we have made with Champions of Caring, and about the amazing service performed by our Champions. She listens, smiles, and holds my hand. Sometimes, she asks if she could come and speak to the students as she used to do. We both know that this is no longer possible, but I love hearing her passion rise through.

The journalist Thomas Friedman wrote a touching op-ed piece in *The New York Times* one Mother's Day. He fondly remembered how a friend once commented that his mother, "put the *mensch* into dementia." I cried when I read this because my mother, even in her most troubling times, when she becomes confused or disorientated, apologizes to all of us, realizing that something is wrong. She says, "Forgive me for not remembering or understanding. I hope that I am not bringing you pain." It's amazing that at this difficult stage in her life, she is still concerned that she is being a *mensch*. How blessed my family and I have been to be taught about life and dignity from my mother—my true Champion.

In January 2009, I lost my husband and dearest friend, Larry. During this painful time of grieving, I have been blessed to have my work with Champions of Caring to keep me connected to people, and provide a sense of purpose and meaning in my life. In helping others, I have truly helped *myself*. Having my own cause keeps me youthful, energetic, interested, and interesting. I have something that I am proud to share with my children, grandchildren, and friends. Champions of Caring makes me want to jump out of bed in the morning. I feel that I am making a contribution, and that I have something to contribute that improves the lives of others, and enables me to live my legacy every day.

I hope that this book has inspired you to start to address your passion to make this a better world. The central message is that as individuals, there may be something—or even *many* things—that each of us can do to overcome the apathy that continues to allow terrible things to occur to our fellow human beings. We can take control of our actions and behaviors in our own corner of the world and make a world of difference. The novelist George Eliot said that "Our deeds determine us as much as we determine our deeds." She also said that "It is never too late to be what you might have been." We can change our lives in ways we may never have imagined. And while we are doing all that, we can *inspire* others to do the same.

RESOURCES AND SUGGESTED READING

Books

Bolles, Richard Nelson. *What Color Is Your Parachute?*, 2006 Edition. Ten Speed Press, 2006.

Bornstein, David. *How to Change the World: Social Entrepreneurs and the Power of New Ideas*. Oxford University Press, 2004.

Clinton, Bill. *Giving*. Alfred A. Knopf, 2007.

Epstein, Helen. *Children of the Holocaust: Conversations With Sons and Daughters of Survivors*. Putnam, 1979.

Freedman, Marc. *Encore: Finding Work that Matters in the Second Half of Life*. Public Affairs, 2007.

Kurshan, Rabbi Neil. *Raising Your Child to Be a Mensch*. Ivy Books, 1987.

Moulden, Julia. *We Are the New Radicals: A Manifesto for Reinventing Yourself and Saving the World*. McGraw Hill, 2008.

Sedlar, Jeri and Miners, Rick. *Don't Retire, Rewire*, Second Edition. Alpha Books, 2007.

Seligman, Martin. *Authentic Happiness: Using the Power of Positive Psychology to Realize Your Potential for Lasting Fulfillment*. Free Press, Simon and Schuster, 2002.

Short Stories

"The Suit," Norman Doidge. *Beyond Imagination: Canadians Write About the Holocaust*. Edited by Grafstein, Jerry S. McClelland & Stewart Inc, 1995.

Articles

"Call Your Mother," Thomas Friedman. New York Times, May 11, 2008.

Web sites

Serve.gov
President Obama's new initiative for national service.

Volunteer Match
volunteermatch.org
A free online service that matches you to volunteer opportunities.

Idealist
idealist.org
Listing of local and global paid and volunteer jobs.

VolunTourism
Voluntourism.org
Provides information about volunteer opportunities abroad.

International Young Professionals Foundation
iypf.org
A not-for-profit that connects young professionals from over 130 countries who want to make a difference.

Encore
encorecareers.org

Civic Ventures
civicventures.org
Information for retirees and baby boomers about finding work that matters in the second part of life.

The Corporation for National and Community Service
getinvolved.gov
Information about national service organizations.

The Skoll Foundation
skollfoundation.org

The Schwab Foundation for Social Entrepreneurship
schwabfound.org,
Information about social entrepreneurship.

Ashoka
ashoka.org
The global association of the world's leading social entrepreneurs.

Youth Service America
ysa.org
Opportunities for youth to create service projects and engage in volunteer activities.

What Kids Can Do
whatkidscando.org
Examples of what young people are doing to change the world.

Champions of Caring
www.championsofcaring.org
The not-for-profit organization that Barbara Greenspan Shaiman founded to teach youth to become social activists.

Embrace Your Legacy
www.embrace-your-legacy.com
Speeches, workshops and consulting services to create leaders for social change.

About Barbara Greenspan Shaiman

Throughout her career, Barbara has been an educator, businesswoman and a social entrepreneur, using her skills to create social change.

She began her career as teacher, developing curriculum for at-risk youth, and later directed Eisenbud & Associates, an executive search firm that specialized in recruiting physicians and healthcare executives nationally. As a leader in this field, she presented frequently on human resources issues at conferences.

In 1995, she founded Champions of Caring (championsofcaring.org) a non-profit organization that has empowered over 10,000 youth in Philadelphia and South Africa to become leaders in service and active, engaged citizens.

Barbara is the daughter of Holocaust survivors. Her mother is the sole survivor of a family of sixty five people, and her father worked for Oskar Schindler, on whose story Steven Spielberg's film *Schindler's List* was based. This family legacy, coupled with her professional experience and work with Champions of Caring, have motivated Barbara to help others to live their legacies by giving back to their communities. Barbara has created programs that have inspired and empowered youth with the skills to create service projects to address local and global issues and create cultures of caring in their schools and communities.

With her strong background in human resources, entrepreneurial spirit, and over thirty years of experience in public speaking, Barbara created **Embrace Your Legacy** to share her message and encourage adults to embrace and live their legacies. Through speeches, workshops and consulting, she shares her highly effective and replicable ten step approach to provide participants with the tools to create social change in an informed and creative way. She has presented this message to audiences of all ages and backgrounds, locally, nationally and internationally.

Barbara holds a BA in psychology and education from Hunter College in New York City, and a master's degree in education from North Adams (Massachusetts) State College. She has received numerous awards for her contributions, including the U.S. Department of Housing and Urban Development "Best Practices Award", the National Association of Women Business Owners "Women Making History Award", State Farm Insurance "Service-Learning Practitioner Award", The Archdiocese of Philadelphia "Servant of God" Award, the Association of Jewish Holocaust Survivors "Mordechai Anielewicz Award", and the Daily Points of Light Award. She has also been inducted into the Hunter College Hall of Fame, named a "Community Quarterback" by the NFL's Philadelphia Eagles and Parade Magazine, and chosen as a "Citizen Hero" by the Philadelphia Inquirer.

Barbara, who resides outside of Philadelphia, speaks five languages and loves to travel. Her children and grandchildren are her greatest joys. Her mother, Carola Greenspan, now in her eighties, continues to be her deepest source of inspiration.

Embrace Your Legacy Speeches, Workshops and Consulting Services

Through **Embrace Your Legacy**, Barbara motivates individuals to assess their core values, identify their passion and skill sets and then utilize these assets to take action and create projects for personal growth and social change. Embrace Your Legacy programs create cultures of caring in communities, organizations and/or business environments by developing socially conscious leaders and active citizens.

Barbara is often called upon to share her message at community events, conferences and workshops. Her audiences include corporations, universities, educators, faith-based communities, women's groups, service organizations, trade associations and professional groups. Her message is both inspirational <u>and</u> directed towards motivating people to action.

For more information about Embrace Your Legacy speeches, workshops, and consulting services, please visit www.embrace-your-legacy.com or email info@embrace-your-legacy.com.